# MARY TIGHE

# MARY TIGHE

Miranda O'Connell

SOMERVILLE PRESS

Somerville Press,
Dromore, Bantry,
Co. Cork, Ireland

Designed by Jane Stark
seamistgraphics@gmail.com
Typeset in Adobe Garamond


ISBN: 978 0 9573461 2 3


Printed and bound in Spain by
GraphyCems, Villatuerta, Navarra

*For Antony Hurst*

# CONTENTS

# ACKNOWLEDGEMENTS

Many people have helped me in the writing of this book. Firstly, I am grateful to Antony Hurst who accompanied me on my research in counties Wicklow and Kilkenny and who advised me about historical background. He also was my patient reader and listener. Without the assistance of Antony Tighe, I would not have made progress: he shared his family records with me. And I am grateful to Bruce Arnold and Mavis Arnold who gave me encouragement and advice whenever I asked and set me out on course to do research. The staff of The British Library, The National Library of Ireland, The National Gallery of Ireland, The Public Records Office of Northern Ireland and the Librarian of The Royal College of Physicians all helped me find the material out of which this book is made. Anne Hamilton of Hamwood House, Co. Meath, Philip Emmet of Altidore, Co. Wicklow, Patricia Butler of The Dower House, Rossana, and John Kirwan gave me information and advice, as did Professor Harriet Kramer Linkin, Dr A.P.W. Malcomson and Seamus Corballis of Kilkenny. Peter Forsaith of Westminster College, Oxford gave assistance with the history of the painting of John Wesley preaching at Rossana, Professor Nicholas Roe advised me on the chapter on Keats, and Professor Roy Foster did the same on the chapter on the 1798 Rebellion. Sinead McCarthy of Browne Architects, Dublin researched four houses and drew a map.

At a more personal level I would like to thank Rebecca O'Connell and Pauline Fitzpatrick who helped with research. Sylvia Webber, Ruth Jackman and Brian Carroll gave help and encouragement. Richard Holmes inspired me in the first place at the University of East Anglia and I am grateful to him for that and to Kathryn Hughes who did the same.

And I am very grateful too to my friends and family who have always urged me on my way with their encouragement.

# FOREWORD

Biography is a great art form, difficult and complex in its construction but in its realisation laying before us a recreated life into which its author has breathed emotional and intellectual reality. It is this, when it works, that makes it creative, close in many ways to fiction. In fiction, the use of real people, modified and generally enhanced in their impact, is accepted. We trace back Micawber to the father of Charles Dickens, Levin in *Anna Karenina* to Tolstoy himself, and so on. In biography we witness the building up of rounded characters often from flat prescriptions, the lives drawn from what is often a paucity of material. This is the first problem to be faced by the biographer and it was very real when first faced by Miranda O'Connell.

When a biographer starts work, there are inevitable gaps in time in the narrative that cannot be explained. There are actions by the subject that have to be discovered and presented convincingly. And quite often, most distressingly of all, there are different expressions of prejudice against the subject that have to be confronted with a rebuilding of the factual material that is available, combined with a fresh investigation of the truthful version of the life lived. All these problems faced the author of *Mary Tighe*. Her subject was largely a lost cause and Mary Tighe had to be rescued from both obscurity and misrepresentation.

Miranda O'Connell brought to her task the right qualities in the right order. She taught English Literature in a Sixth Form College in Oxfordshire for a number of years and as she worked, reading and teaching literature to her pupils, she realised she should be writing as well. She then studied with Richard Holmes and Kathryn Hughes on the Creative Writing Course at the University of East Anglia. The work for her M.A. dissertation took her forward in the journey into biography in two significant ways that went far beyond the defined achievement of the prescribed task. For her thesis, she recreated an event in the lives of two figures, one a writer, the other a painter. John Millington Synge was the better known of the two and was asked, in 1905 by the *Manchester Guardian,* to travel in the West of Ireland and write for the paper about the Congested Districts Board and how well they were relieving poverty in Connemara and Mayo. He was invited by C.P. Scott, the editor, to accept the help and companionship as illustrator of the Irish artist, Jack Yeats, who agreed to accompany him. As a result, twelve vivid and poignant articles appeared as an illustrated series in what was at the time a great campaigning newspaper. They have remained a powerful description of poverty and want among a proud peasant people.

Miranda O'Connell brought to life the journey undertaken by Synge and Jack Yeats and in so doing she took from this task two very important requirements in the writing of biography. The first was to describe and animate the binding human relationship that developed between the two men. Biography depends on that bringing together of characters, often on the basis of sparse facts. The second was the importance of knowing the landscape and the environment. She travelled where the Irish playwright and his artist companion went on their journey in Connemara, trying to find the circumstances of the lives Yeats and Synge were describing for *Manchester Guardian* readers in England.

This early experience made the translation from the wilds of Connemara and Mayo to the rich countryside around Inistioge and the rather different wildness of County Wicklow a successful one. The author writes well of the social milieu and the landscape and brings to the life of Mary Tighe the significance of the territory that inspired her and from which she derived the material for her lyrical writing on love, most notably in her greatest poem, 'Psyche; or, The Legend of Love'.

Much physical material of the life the poet led has survived. Her mausoleum, with its fine Flaxman sculpture of the recumbent woman, remains in the churchyard at Inistioge. Two fine estates on which she spent parts of her life survive in Wicklow and Kilkenny. And there is of course Marsh's library where her father, Revd William Blachford, was librarian and where Mary Tighe was born. To a remarkable degree, with some exceptions, the world she inhabited stands largely unspoiled. In writing biography, familiarity with the places, direct forceful understanding of the full scene is vital anyway but is richly important when places are preserved in a state that reasonably approximates to what the subject of the life experienced.

The emotional material of the life of the poet has survived in a different way. Early biographers found it difficult to gain access to family members or to collect material from which her story could be told. Nevertheless, portraits of close relations have been discovered as well as contemporary painted views and these, together with letters and family reminiscences, illuminate the account. There was a more sombre stage in the journey of realising a woman poet's life in the late eighteenth and early nineteenth centuries. Mary Tighe faced many difficulties and misrepresentations, not just in her own life but in the judgments people made about her and in the subsequent fate posterity bestowed on her.

The most obvious example is in the impact Mary Tighe made on John Keats. This was not inconsiderable. In her greatest poem she inspired in others, including Keats, a recognition of the undying magic of the legend of Cupid and Psyche, taken by her from *The Golden Ass* by Apuleius. Keats, deservedly, became the glory of English romantic poetry. Mary Tighe was unfairly diminished by Harry Buxton Forman in his 1883 four-volume edition of Keats to a marginal and passing influence: 'the authoress of the now almost forgotten poem of Psyche' is reduced to being 'an indication of the poet's taste in verse at this period'. Yet Keats named her in one poem and Miranda O'Connell devotes a chapter to a significant and balanced assessment of the influence of the woman poet, twenty-three years his senior, on John Keats. One does not lightly engage in a reassessment of such a figure as Keats but this is an occasion for such a task of collecting the true version of the facts and it is done in the best tradition of balanced literary criticism.

A leading authority today on Irish poetry of the period, familiar with much of Mary Tighe's work, told me he rated 'Psyche: or, The Legend of Love' a great poem and that her sonnets are wonderful examples of the form.

Miranda O'Connell engages with the question of the poet's 'secret grief' and looks in detail at the significant relationships in her life, considering as well the part they played in the writing of 'Psyche'. The great enemy, most tragic of all, was poor health. Mary Tighe was a consumptive and her illness is considered against the background of the tuberculosis epidemic of the eighteenth and nineteenth centuries as she endured a slow, unhappy decline without her harp or her poems to comfort her at the end.

By that stage in the Life, one has discovered nobility and talent, creative genius and a calm aspect towards suffering. Mary Tighe has been brought back to life and she excites our admiration and our involvement in her not inconsiderable achievement as a poet. She departs a rounded and fully drawn figure from the caring and discriminating hands of her biographer.

*Bruce Arnold*

# INTRODUCTION
## *Mary Blachford Tighe*

There is an oral tradition in the village of Inistioge, Co.Kilkenny that on 23 March 1810 Mary Tighe rose from her sickbed in the drawing room at Woodstock, her cousin William's estate, where she had spent the last few months after moving there in the summer of 1809. Independent by nature, she hated to feel cut off from life and realised she was in some senses a prisoner. It was a bright day, so she set out on her own into the gardens and started to make her way down the path which sloped (and slopes still) off the drive to the right and on into the woods. From here it was possible to cross over the side of the hill and descend gently, pausing to see the slow silver water slip under the many-arched stone bridge over the River Nore. In the distance the square tower of the church stood stolidly against the backdrop of green fields, and the woods rolled beyond to the horizon. Perhaps the primroses were already out – touches of yellow in the woods and in the cottage gardens of the village. But soon, they say in Inistioge, as she turned to go home, her strength left her. Her breath was shallow at the best of times but now she gasped and fell recumbent on green grass that was not yet warmed by full sun since it was early in the year. As she waited, she thought of her father, long dead. The servants found her quickly – her absence had already stirred the house to action – and they carried her tenderly back to the drawing room where she lay with her head cushioned on the bolster of the couch, her chin in the palm of her hand.

*The tomb of Mary Tighe at Inistioge by John Flaxman*

It is thus that she is portrayed in an effigy of Portland stone upon her tomb, for Mary Tighe died in the early hours of 24 March 1810. In the common churchyard at Inistioge surrounded by rusty wire and railings is an old tower and nearby is her burial place: the heavy cube of a mausoleum rises with imperious severity and classical grace from the tumble of gravestones around. Weeds grow to the door which is seldom opened and few ask for her by name. Here she lies, hidden from the eye. The glance falls on the statue by John Flaxman of Mary Tighe: she reclines, elegant head in the crook of her elbow. Her face is turned towards the intruder and raised upwards. The heavy eyes and composed mouth suggest inner contemplation and she seems totally at peace. The marble gown floats down the long body towards her cold feet and at her head, hand on cheek in serious thought as he watches his charge, stands a small winged figure. He seems to have perched on her shoulder. Is this a reference to the winged Cupid of her poem about Psyche? Perhaps he is the angel

*The mausoleum in the churchyard at Inistioge by Michael Craig*

sometimes depicted by the sculptor Flaxman, a guardian who watches over the living and the dead, a testament to the virtuous life? Or maybe this is the genius of poetry. The sculptured memorial pays tribute to a poet with a wide readership in the nineteenth century, yet today her name has mysteriously disappeared from most of our poetry anthologies.

The 'disappearance' of Mary Tighe began quite soon after her death, as is revealed by the account of her tenacious biographer, William Howitt in *Homes and Haunts of the British Poets* (published in 1847 and revised in 1894). In the opening passages of his essay (where she is in excellent company amongst the great poets – Chaucer, Spenser, Shakespeare, Cowley,

Milton, to name the first five), Howitt comments 'perhaps no writer of merit has been more neglected by her own friends than Mary Tighe. With every means of giving to the public a good memoir of her, I believe no such is in existence; at all events, I have not been able to find one'. Howitt goes on to highlight the difficulty of writing a biography where neglect and the passage of time have concealed vital facts. He speaks of 'strangely clashing accounts of a popular poetess' and he himself set out for Ireland to find the truth of the matter. However, he was refused admittance at her chief places of residence, Rossana, Co. Wicklow, and Woodstock, Co. Kilkenny, having come all the way from England, and even at 'Innerstiogue' at her mausoleum he could gather little by way of facts. After quite some research and correspondence, Howitt found that the tradition that Mary Tighe died on a couch on her return from a walk and was portrayed by Flaxman in that same position on her tomb had no foundation. A close family member (Mrs Elinor Ward, daughter of a first cousin of Mary Tighe) told him that Mary had 'lost all power of movement in her legs and feet and was carried from room to room.' But Mary did go out that March, for her first cousin wrote in her last letter to her '. . . we cannot help thinking that you were a little venturesome in driving out so early in the year'. Myth and memory mingle and the biographer must unravel the tangles.

Howitt was not granted an interview with a member of the family at either Rossana or Woodstock:

> In every other case, so invariably have I found the most obliging facilities given for the prosecution of my inquiries, that I have long ceased to carry a letter of introduction; my name, of twenty-three years' standing before the public, being considered warranty enough. I found it equally so in Ireland, except with the Tighes.

Howitt's adverse comments reflect his belief that the family had rejected their poet:

> They were ashamed, probably, that any of their name should have degraded herself by writing poetry, which a man or woman without an acre may do.

The family had neglected the mausoleum as well, which confirmed his view:

In the wall at the back of the monument, aloft, there is an oblong-square hole left for for the inscription, which I understood was lying about at the house, but no single effort had been made to put it up, though it would not require an hour's work and though Mrs Tighe has been dead six-and-thirty years.

Thus it would appear that less than forty years after her death, Mary Tighe was almost forgotten by the local community where she had died, and inquiries about her were unwelcome, as William Howitt discovered when he walked, notebook in hand, in the footsteps of the woman whose biography he sought to write.

The poet's major work, 'Psyche; or, The Legend of Love', was completed in 1802. A limited edition of fifty copies was published privately in 1805 and copies were given to a number of her friends, including Thomas Moore, Eleanor Butler, Sarah Ponsonby, William Parnell and Anna Seward. There were many further requests for a reprint but nothing happened within her short life.

However, a year after her death, Longmans published thirty-nine of her short poems together with 'Psyche; or, The Legend of Love'. Between 1811 and 1853 there were seven multiple editions of *Psyche* and the first run at Longmans sold 500 copies in a month. A short and tiny book was privately published in 1811 entitled *Mary, a Series of Reflections during Twenty Years*. Her work was positively and frequently reviewed from 1811 onwards and the great brigade of critical monthlies – *The British Critic, The British Review, The Critical Review, The Eclectic Review, The Glasgow Magazine, The Gentlemen's Magazine, The Monthly Review, The Poetical Register* and *The Quarterly Review* – published articles on *Psyche* between 1811 and 1813. In 1819 John Wilson of *Blackwood's Edinburgh Magazine* commented: 'Scotland has her Baillie – Ireland her Tighe – England her Hemans'. Many of her poems were circulated privately and turn up today in unexpected places; for example, in the papers of her London doctor at The Royal College of Physicians or amongst the letters of the Ladies of Llangollen. *Selena*, her long novel about the vagaries of social life, was published in 2012 for the very first time.

She influenced Felicia Hemans, Lord Byron, Percy Bysshe Shelley, Mary Shelley, Thomas Moore, Sydney Owenson (Lady Morgan), Elizabeth Barrett Browning, Charlotte Brontë, Edgar Allan Poe, Emily Dickinson and Christina Rossetti. The first of Keats's famous Odes is entitled 'Ode to Psyche'. In his works are to be found numerous echoes of her poems, for in his early years, John Keats read Mary Tighe's work often. He mentions her in one of his poems of 1817 and he later copied one of her sonnets to send to his brother in America. This sonnet was eventually published as Keats's own work in H.Buxton Forman's edition of 1883 and remained there unchallenged for many years. More famously, in a letter to George and Georgiana Keats, Keats rejected Mary Tighe saying that she was no longer an influence upon him. He had outgrown her: it is this negative aspect of her reputation that has survived. And in the twentieth century her work went out of print. Today a selection of her work is to be found in anthologies of romantic poetry by editors such as Duncan Wu and Jonathan Wordsworth and an edition of her poetry was published in America in 2005. A few stanzas have made their way into *The Penguin Book of Irish Poetry* and an extract from a poem appeared on an Oxbridge finals paper. But very few students knew who she was.

Mary Tighe was born in Dublin on 9 October 1772. Her father, the Reverend William Blachford, was Prebendary of Howth and St Patrick's Cathedral and Keeper and Librarian of Marsh's Library, Dublin; her mother, daughter of William Tighe of Rossana, Co. Wicklow, was descended from the Earls of Darnley. Just seven months after the birth of his daughter, William Blachford died suddenly and the baby and her infant brother were taken to live for a number of years at Altidore Castle in the hills above Greystones in County Wicklow, her father's family home. Her mother, Theodosia Blachford, educated both children to a high standard but once they reached their teens their family life was peripatetic as they moved between Dublin and friends' homes in the country. Adored but over-protected by an anxious single mother, as a young woman Mary danced her way round Dublin and London, going to the theatre for the first time, to Vauxhall Gardens and visiting with the best. For reasons she seems little to have understood, she married Henry Tighe, her first cousin, in 1793, aged not quite twenty-one. She regretted her decision immediately and for the next few years interrogated herself relentlessly. Why had she done such a thing? But then she became ill and her life changed. She visited various doctors in England and went to spas and watering places where it was hoped her health would improve. But she wanted to write and it took her insidiously advancing illness to bring her back to the little room in the attic at the family home where she could be alone, or to the cottage which Henry had built for her close by in the grounds. Here, in the house called Rossana, in which both her mother and her husband had been born, she wrote her major works and today it still sits on the banks of the Vartry in County Wicklow. A petrified shell in beautiful grounds is all that is left of Woodstock, the great house at Inistioge which belonged to her husband's brother, and where Mary Tighe died of tuberculosis before she was forty.

The Tighes had come to Ireland from Lincolnshire in the mid-seventeenth century. They settled quickly and within a generation had bought the estate at Rossana and property in Dublin too. Life in Georgian times was prosperous when Mary was a girl, as is evidenced in the elegant, confident style of domestic architecture which reflects the scale on which life in the capital was lived. Street upon street of handsome town houses graced the city. The grandeur of buildings such as The Custom House, Trinity College and the Four Courts reflects a huge confidence in the infrastructure that supported society.

As she danced at night at Dublin Castle balls and took her carriage back to the Tighe family house in Dominick Street, Mary was only just aware of the economic fluctuations that were shaking her country, and she scarcely understood the power of the secret societies of United Irishmen which were moving towards outright rebellion as they were driven underground by legislation, nor the complex reasons why Ireland was beginning to change. She knew of the French Revolution. Her aunt and mother-in-law had seen King Louis XVI in Paris in 1787, had ogled him at supper with the royal family, as the public were allowed to do, and they had doubtless heard of the American struggle for independence.

But Mary Blachford would not have expected the people of Ireland to gather their powers so effectively and to challenge the authority of the ruling Protestants in the 1798 Rebellion. Nor would she have foreseen that Britain would react so nervously and call for the Act of Union of 1801 by which Ireland became an integrated part of the United Kingdom, ending for the time being Grattan's Parliament and Ireland's small taste of measured independence. The great gilded carapace of the Protestant ruling class, the Ascendancy, was starting to crack, at first with little tremors of weakness, but by the time of Mary's death in March 1810 with a dull roar. There was a decline in confidence felt within Irish society at large. The Tighe family at Rossana were for a time forced to barricade their doors against the rebels and they, like other landowners, had to question where their allegiance lay: Mary's husband, Henry, found his mission in the 1798 Rebellion as he led his men up into the hills of Wicklow and challenged the rebels, while Mary took into the house a Catholic working man who had been attacked. There is a special appeal in this story of a young woman who lived at a point in history where one era seems to tremble and topple over to become another: the wealth and confidence of the Enlightenment was slipping into the age of the new Romanticism, with its emphasis on personal freedom rather than ordered rationalism.

The Tighes were of the landed gentry in Ascendancy Ireland and their social contacts were many and are well documented in their journals and letters. Mary was a firm friend of the poet Thomas Moore who wrote a poem entitled 'To Mrs Henry Tighe, On Reading her "Psyche"':

> *Tell me that witching tale again,*
> *For never has my heart or ear*
> *Hung on so sweet, so pure a strain,*
> *So pure to feel, so sweet to hear.*

Felicia Hemans wrote several poems as tributes to Mary after her death. The Tighes had close family links with one of the two young ladies of Llangollen, both Irish women, who ran away from their homes in County Kilkenny and set up their own establishment in Wales. Their dramatic escape from the miseries of the marriage market in Ascendancy Ireland must have seemed pertinent to Mary's own situation. She visited Eleanor Butler and Sarah Ponsonby in Llangollen where they lived on their own farm which they ran with strict and cheerful economy. Stories were told in the family of Cousin George Tighe, who went on the Grand Tour and met in Rome Margaret Mountcashel, a countess, whose childhood and teenage years on her family's Irish estate had been enhanced by her governess – Mary Wollstonecraft. Margaret became a political pamphleteer who corresponded with William Godwin and she took George William Tighe as her lover, abandoning her husband, Earl Mountcashel.

And one of Mary's uncles was a clergyman with a living in the Mourne Mountains who sponsored the young Parick Brontë when he was still called Patrick Brunty. John Wesley and his brother Charles stayed at Rossana when they were in the Wicklow area. John wrote some of his sermons there, while Charles composed and played hymns on the organ especially installed for him in the Long Room. Arthur Wellesley (who was to become the Duke of Wellington) visited the Tighe's Dominick Street house in Dublin, as did William Parnell, whose estate at Avondale was on the way to Rossana and Woodstock. Mary's portrait was painted by George Romney, as was that of her cousin William Tighe while he was at Eton.

Mary Tighe's sonnets are amongst the finest of her poems. They show her experience of life conveyed with mastery of form and expression. As William Howitt presciently realised, the story of her life was soon lost. Why has her work been so long neglected? Why is she hidden still in her locked mausoleum? Mary Tighe's voice was once clear and strong and she asks to be heard once again.

# CHAPTER 1

# THE EARLY YEARS
## *'How bright the lustre'*

Mary Blachford was born on 9 October 1772 in Dublin to Theodosia, wife of the librarian of Marsh's Library, William Blachford. It seems likely that she spent the first seven months of her life in the residential ground floor apartments of the building near St Patrick's Cathedral from where her father ascended the steps each morning to the beautiful first-floor rooms. The library remains to this day much as it was at the time of Mary's birth; the bookcases are tall and finely carved, the high windows throw light into the book-lined room. Mary's older brother John, born a year earlier in 1771, had memories of the pretty garden and pools of grass and his father's morning departure to work upstairs and of the library itself where the dark oak bookcases formed narrow gated reading-booths into which scholars were locked to prevent them from stealing the books.

But William Blachford died of a fever when his daughter was only seven months old and the happy life of this small Dublin family came to an abrupt end. The sudden curtailment of good fortune threw a shadow across the life of Mary Blachford even at so young an age. From now on, after a period of her childhood spent at her father's country home, she moved from one place to another, supported by her relatives but never able to call any house her own.

Mary's life began at Marsh's Library and her love of reading was to be one of its most important aspects. Her father, Prebendary of Howth and

*Marsh's Library*

of Tasgarret, was a successful, indeed exemplary keeper of the city's most famous library. He worked at Marsh's for seven years with the wide range of 25,000 books bequeathed to this place of learning, of which Jonathan Swift had been the Governor for many years. William Blachford was the eldest son of Dr John Blachford, a wealthy property owner who was Chancellor of St Patrick's Cathedral in Dublin and Rector of St Werburgh's. His mother was Elinor, daughter of the Acton family of Wicklow. It was to the family estate, Altidore Castle at Kilpedder, near Greystones, Co. Wicklow, that Theodosia Blachford and her small children at first withdrew on his death.

Designed and perhaps built by Lovett Pearce in the 1720s, Altidore sits in the hills above Kilpedder and appears today much as when Mary Blachford was a child. Four grand octagonal towers roost amongst the trees and in the time when Mary's paternal grandfather had owned the property, a drive over two miles long wound its way up from the sea at nearby Greystones, dipped and rose along the brow of the hills to the front door which is sheltered from the wind on the landward side.

The house – for it is more of a house than a fort – is built into the slope which falls away below the sitting-room windows and allows a fine uninterrupted view across several green miles to the sea. Bray and Greystones shimmer distantly. From the windows the young Mary traced the route of visitors' carriages as they approached, her finger inscribing their curving path in the mist of her breath on the pane. From the north-facing window she saw the three canals or ponds which, she was told, her father had loved to fish. When William Blachford died suddenly, his wife felt herself to be acutely deprived at the abrupt end of a happy marriage. She decided to remain where she was, for her children were very young and could grow safely at Altidore. When they were a little older, Theodosia Blachford took them to Dublin, to the Tighe house in Dominick Street in the north of the city. But for the time being she felt that the castle in County Wicklow was a kind of sanctuary from which she was at first reluctant to venture. Here she was closest to her husband because it had been his home. Only too soon her growing children would draw her out into the world. There were different levels of the Irish aristocracy and though the Tighes and Blachfords were not of the very grandest rank who often owned more land in England than Ireland, their families held substantial acreages in Ireland. It was normal practice in the eighteenth century for a wealthy family sometimes to rent rather than purchase a property. However, it seems that the restless movement

*Altidore Castle*

of Theodosia, Mary and John is in some way related to their bereavement and symptomatic of a restless search for home. Much later, John would return to towered Altidore when he himself had a family.

Later in her life, it was to Rossana, the Tighe house in which Theodosia was born and grew up, that her daughter Mary constantly returned, for her mother came from the Tighe family, the same into which Mary would one day marry. The Rossana estate was part of the O'Byrne's patrimony before the eighteenth century, but was bought by Richard Tighe in 1741 and remained in the family until the late twentieth century. This grand old house still stands on many acres of land in County Wicklow, near Ashford.

By way of introduction to Rossana, it is interesting to follow the writer William Howitt on his journey in 1845 as he set out for Ireland to undertake research for his life of Mary Blachford Tighe, author of 'Psyche; or, The Legend of Love', with the intention of adding her to his now substantial work, *Homes and Haunts of the British Poets,* which was to be published the following year. He carried with him what he termed 'brief particulars furnished by a private hand' where details of the poet's birth, marriage and death were given in about half a page. Howitt describes his approach to the lovely County Wicklow:

*A view from the drawing room at Altidore*

The whole country round is extremely beautiful, and calculated to call forth the poetic faculty where it exists. All the way from Dublin to Rossana is through a rich and lovely district. As you approach Rossana the hills become higher, and your way lies through the most beautifully wooded valleys. At the inn at Ashford Bridge you have the celebrated Devil's Glen on one hand, and Rossana on the other. This glen lies a mile or more from the inn, and is about a mile and a half through. It is narrow, the hills on either hand are lofty, bold, craggy, and finely wooded; and along the bottom runs, deep and dark over its rocky bed, the River Vartry. This river runs down and crosses the road near the inn, and then takes its way by Rossana. Rossana is perhaps a mile down the valley from the inn. The house is a plain old brick house, fit for a country squire. It lies low in the meadow near the river, and around it, on both sides of the water, the slopes are dotted with the most beautiful and luxuriant trees. The park at Rossana is indeed eminently beautiful with its wood. The trees are thickly scattered, and a great proportion of them are lime, the soft, delicate foliage of which gives a peculiar character to the scenery. The highway, for the whole length of the park as you proceed toward Rathdrum, is completely arched over with magnificent beeches, presenting a fine natural arcade. On the right the ground ascends for a mile or more, covered with rich masses of wood. In fact, whichever way you turn, toward the distant hill, or pursuing your way down the valley, all is one fairyland of beauty and richness. It is a region worthy of the author of 'Psyche', worthy to inspire her beautiful mind; and we rejoice that so fair, gentle, and good spirit had there her lot cast.[1]

Howitt points out that the lands of Rossana are low-lying and, as a child, Theodosia knew the concerns about flooding, for this was where she grew up. The River Vartry ran across the foot of the garden which is splendidly planted with trees, particularly sweet chestnuts. Later, in her poem 'The Vartree' of 1797, her daughter would write of the lawns her mother loved:

> *Sweet are thy banks, O Vartree, when at morn*
> *Their velvet verdure glistens with the dew;*
> *When fragrant gales by softest zephyrs borne*
> *Unfold the flowers and ope the petals new.*

*How bright the lustre of thy silver tide,*
*Which winds, reluctant to forsake the vale!*
*How play the quivering branches on thy side,*
*And lucid catch the sunbeam in the gale!*

*And sweet thy shade at Noon's more fervid hours,*
*When faint, we quit the upland gayer lawn*
*To seek the freshness of thy sheltering bowers,*
*Thy chestnut glooms, where day can scarcely dawn.*[2]

Theodosia had spent her childhood happily at Rossana with her three brothers, Richard, Edward and William, despite the early death of her mother, Lady Mary Bligh, sister to Lord Darnley, and despite the remarriage of her father to Margaret Theaker, whom Theodosia at first disliked but later came to love very much. Theodosia educated herself, in a time before governesses were hired, by using her father's library. When he married again, two more siblings were added to the Tighe family, Thomas and Barbara. Theodosia was required to read to her gouty father for long periods at a time and many books of travels abroad and volumes of history were absorbed in this way, the child taking in some but not all of what she read aloud, and thinking herself unlucky, like Milton's daughters, when she was on the early morning shift and her father insisted she continue through the day. There were books in the library at Rossana on the role of women in society which Theodosia read; she saw her mother's name inscribed in one of them and discovered it contained disappointing advice given by the Marquis of Halifax to his daughter: 'Little is required of an accomplished woman except to make the most of a drunken husband, to learn how to govern a silly one and to manage the house with economy.' Because her own

*Tighe's Avenue, Rossana, Co. Wicklow*

childhood was spent in a family of complex relationships with many demands made for her services, Theodosia resolved to put all her energies into giving her own daughter special opportunities for self-fulfilment in life. Caroline Hamilton, niece to Theodosia, writes in her account of her cousin Mary's childhood: 'The society in which she lived in the early part of her life was calculated, in different ways, to inspire her with a taste for reflection and study.'[3]

Caroline goes on to tell of Theodosia's eagerness to educate her own children to high standards at home. They were not made to execute the curious tasks so beloved of governesses of the period, but were encouraged to read widely and to talk about books. However, John 'did not learn as fast as she thought he should' and so he was despatched to Eton at the age of twelve, where he spent much of his free time alone with his books. Theodosia gave him little pocket money and he became a solitary boy who was obliged to live separately from his schoolfellows. 'He was made unhappy by his mother's too great anxiety,' said Caroline Hamilton. The anxiety was no doubt conveyed if not transferred to the boy, whose sheltered Irish rural education at home with his sister was in strong contrast to the competitive

*Rossana, Co. Wicklow, sketched by Caroline Hamilton in about 1790*

life of boarding school and the hazardous journey across the Irish Sea, which he most often undertook alone. Cousin Caroline remarks, 'It was never with any pleasure that he spoke of the time he spent at Eton'. However, when he was older, John came to be considered a bright student who gained 'every honour' in the University of Dublin (Trinity College) when he took his degree, perhaps because he flourished in his native Ireland.

So when John was safely despatched to Eton, Mary was left alone with her mother. Caroline Hamilton notes that there was no emphasis upon acquiring 'the most correct Parisian accent or even a very good carriage' and she has more to add on the subject of education:

> Many years before any writer on education had dared to call in question the utility of making an unhappy child, learn year after year, columns of spelling from Abbot to Zoology, Mrs Blachford taught spelling by writing. At a very early age Mary's chief employment was copying neatly into blank books, poems and select passages from good authors which were always well chosen as Mrs Blachford had a warm imagination and great feeling which I have heard her daughter say would have made her a literary character if her education and religious principles had not turned her thoughts another way. Besides transcribing from English authors, Mary translated volumes from French, to which I attribute the ease with which she soon learned to write. She committed much poetry to memory, repeating what she learned with much feeling and good taste...[4]

Theodosia's ideas were, in fact, progressive. She believed that children, if well taught when young, would be self-motivated later and learn on their own. She clearly loved her daughter deeply and hoped to do the very best for her, particularly because of the death of the child's father, as she mentions in a memorial to Mary written after her death: 'The promise of beauty, intelligence and vigorous health, which she gave in infancy and a very caressing, & flattering manner, naturally endeared her peculiarly to me and inspired me with the brightest hopes respecting her future destiny.'[5]

Theodosia Blachford was a scrupulously careful parent, always believing that she must watch over the young to protect them from the influence of the world. She had been converted to Methodism during this period,

*Theodosia, Mary and John Blachford painted by Theodosia Blachford, 1780*

when John Wesley paid many visits to Ireland: he stayed with the Tighe family at Rossana for it was his habit to use the houses of the wealthy as a base from which to go out to preach to the poor. His doctrine of simplicity and discipline appealed to those like Theodosia who were in retreat from eighteenth-century extravagance. Irish landlords were not noted for their abstinence and there is no doubt but that Theodosia reacted to the sensuality of the age in a way that affected the upbringing of her children. As a small girl, Mary accepted her mother's solicitude but in some senses the pattern of her life can be seen as a struggle for flight away from such cramping restraint. Moreover, the loss of William Blachford so early in Mary's childhood was an affliction for both mother and daughter and one that neither of them fully understood. Theodosia tells of 'a very extraordinary dream'[6] that her daughter had as early as seven years old. She dreamed of the Day of Judgement, of Jesus leading the good into heaven and a devil dragging others down to Hell. Mary wrote of her childhood vision: 'I thought I saw my father in a white robe coming to me, and my mama and brother without robes, arm in arm, who told me we should be happy; which so delighted that it awoke me, and I was sorry to find it was only a dream.' [7]

The child acknowledges the impact of her father's death in her poignant and significant dream, but Theodosia only just this once refers in her journal to what had happened and she certainly made few allowances in her treatment of her daughter. The tone of self-rebuke in this passage about Mary's early childhood is very pronounced:

> My attachment at this time to my sweet child, was very weak in comparison to what it was in after years. Indeed, I do not think I loved her as much as most mothers would have loved such a child, and certainly saw her faults in a strong light and reproved them with severity, the more on account of religious profession. [8]

It is clear that Mary's relationship with her mother was conditioned by a curious mixture of firmness and even severity, as well as a profound affection. The widow found the tenets of Methodism supported her when times were difficult and she encouraged her children to embrace the faith.

The extended Tighe family provided several other fairly close relationships with adults and, from an early age, Mary enjoyed the company of her mother's three brothers, William, Edward and Richard Tighe, which to some extent compensated for the loss of her father. The eldest uncle, William, 'universally admired for the uprightness of his character and beloved for his courteous manner', distinguished himself at Eton and at Cambridge. He published a letter to his uncle Lord Darnley on the injury which Ireland sustained from absentees, *A letter to Lord Darnley on the state of the poor in Ireland, 1781*. However, perhaps the favourite of Mary's uncles was Edward, who 'lived much with the actors and wits of his day'. Somewhat unpredictable because of his various eccentricities, Edward wrote on the abuse of whiskey and potatoes, which he considered was the cause of the misery of the degradation of the Irish. It was he who advised that Theodosia should give up the effort to educate the young John Blachford at home and send him away to school at Eton. A much more worldly, extroverted character than his sister, Edward influenced his niece in that he gave her a sense of enjoyment in the simple rituals of life. Rossana was a house renowned for good conversation and pleasure in the daily round.

The youngest uncle, Richard, was a tranquil, religious man and more like Theodosia. It was he who introduced Theodosia to discussion of the spiritual life, preparing her for the time in 1777 when she would be introduced to Methodism by her artist friend, Henry Brooke. And Thomas, Theodosia's half-brother, was often away at school at Harrow in England and then at St John's College, Cambridge. He became a strong Methodist, was ordained and appointed to two parishes in the north of Ireland, Drumgooland and Drumballyroney in County Down. A generous and hospitable man, Thomas Tighe encouraged and helped one Patrick Brunty, a young countryman born in a single-roomed cabin, to go into the church by sending him to Cambridge. At this point, Mr Brunty changed his name to Brontë; his passage to Yorkshire and to the parsonage at Haworth is well known because three of his daughters, Charlotte, Anne and Emily, took up their pens and wrote novels.

The influence of these maternal uncles upon the young and fatherless Mary was considerable and the dilemmas she later experienced as a young woman seeking to choose between a society life of pleasure and a more retired, scholarly existence spring from this time spent amongst her close family. So carefully raised by a mother with the best of intentions, she proved a highly strung and sometimes wilful young woman.

The city of Dublin in which Mary grew up in the Tighe family house in Dominick Street was prosperous and Dubliners were conscious from 1782, when Grattan's Parliament was formed, of being empowered in a new sense. Ireland was not economically independent of Britain, but at least parliament was situated in Dublin, not London, and reforms were promised which would eventually enfranchise Catholics. In the wider countryside, farmers such as those of County Wicklow, were enjoying the benefits of a boom. The far west and other very rural areas may have continued to be excluded from the new prosperity, but the building of turnpike roads radiating from Dublin allowed landowners to send their beef to the English markets where a good price could always be obtained. In some areas the agricultural sector was thriving. However, the inherent tensions of Ireland, the essentially insecure position of the Anglo-Irish, the war in America and the French Revolution all made their impact on the world of Ascendancy politics which had seemed so impregnable up until now. In 1792 some civil rights were given to Catholics. 'Defender' societies, secret societies formed to protect the rights of Catholics, campaigned openly and the United Irishmen grew more republican as their ideas were turned towards action by Theobald Wolfe Tone, the Kildare Protestant whose leadership gave new power to the emergent revolutionary movement. And there were many reasons why countrymen and women who knew little of such societies might have cause for grievance: they were poor, had little to eat and too many tithes to pay. The fuel for the fire of the 1798 Rebellion was kindling towards the point of ignition. The political tension arose within the period from 1770 to 1801, the first thirty years of Mary Tighe's life.

NOTES

1   William Howitt: *Homes and Haunts of the British Poets*, Routledge, 1847 and 1894.
2   'The Vartree' by Mary Tighe, 1797.
3   Caroline Hamilton: *Mary Tighe*,  NLI 4810.
4   ibid.
5   Theodosia Blachford: *Observations on the Journal of Mary Tighe*, NLI 4810.
6   Theodosia Blachford: *Observations on the Journal of Mary Tighe*, NLI 4810.
7   *Mary Tighe, A Series of Reflections during Twenty Years*, Roundwood, 1811, NLI LO373.
8   Theodosia Blachford: *Observations on the Journal of Mary Tighe*, NLI 4810.

# CHAPTER 2

# MEETING WITH COUSINS

## *'Dear chestnut bower'*

The widow Theodosia Blachford was determined to be a good parent to her children and she had the wealth and status to implement her wishes. So she stayed on in the security of towered Altidore during her children's infancy. And eventually she took them to Rossana to meet their Tighe cousins, initiating in Mary a deep and binding affection for the old house near the river where her mother had grown up. Theodosia seemed hardly to intend that there should

*Rossana, Co. Wicklow, by Lucy Tighe, 1900*

be a strong bond between her daughter and nephews and nieces but before she saw the need for Mary to break away, the cables of friendship and then of love had become too strong to be broken. How could she persuade her daughter away from a natural sense of kinship and affinity?

Rossana is the house that most profoundly affects this story. It stands today, an elegant reflection of its warm and glorious self amidst ancient trees with gnarled and crooked branches, one of which is the chestnut under which John Wesley preached a famous sermon. Working in the service of Cromwell, Richard Tighe had come from Market Deeping in Lincolnshire to Ireland in the mid-seventeenth century and became Sheriff of Dublin and Mayor as well as MP for the city. He gradually acquired estates in counties Carlow, Dublin and Westmeath but it was not until about a hundred years later that the Tighes found land on which to build a home for the generations to come. Mary Blachford's grandfather, William Tighe, built Rossana and it was finished in 1743. The house remained in the family until the end of the twentieth century. In 1765 the son of the man who built the house, also called William, Theodosia's brother, married Sarah Fownes. William Tighe of Rossana, MP for Athboy, Co. Meath, in 1761 and later for Wicklow, considered himself a very happy man for not only was he master of the treasured Rossana, but he had also acquired the estate of Woodstock, Co. Kilkenny, by his marriage to Sarah Fownes, an only child. Their marriage was a happy one and they had five children, first cousins to Mary Blachford: the sons were William, Henry and John and the daughters, Elizabeth and Caroline Tighe. The two elder sons were those with whom Mary's life was to become interwoven, not just as first cousins through propinquity of blood, but in other more significant ways. The third son, John, probably did not survive his teenage years. His death is not recorded. Though the two elder boys were close in their relationship with one another, their characters were in marked contrast because their upbringing had been very different – a fact that affected their lives deeply. Their sister Caroline married into the Hamilton family of County Meath and it is her records of family life which inform much of this story. She remained close to her cousin Mary all her life.

Sarah, mother to the five Tighe children who were cousins to Mary Blachford, was the only child of Sir William and Lady Fownes and through this marriage the great Palladian mansion and estate at Woodstock, Inistioge, Co. Kilkenny, came into the Tighe family. The eighteenth-century Tighes were powerful landlords in their own right but even more so when joined in marriage to the Fownes, and Sarah liked to remind her Tighe relations of this fact. Her childhood home was a short drive from the village of Inistioge and was set in landscaped gardens and a park. Acres of family woods and farmland surrounded the property but today the house stares with rows of eyes like the sockets of a skull: nothing remains except the outer walls and empty window frames. The graciousness of Ascendancy architecture has fled, for in 1922 Woodstock was looted and burnt by the IRA because it had been used as a barracks for the Black and Tans. Today the gardens have been beautifully replanted with grants from Bord Fáilte and in the abyss between the blighted façade of the mansion and the assiduous restoration of the grounds lies the crux of Irish history.

For the widowed Theodosia, visits to Rossana were feasible. The distance down to Ashford from Kilpedder was not too great to be undertaken in the

*Woodstock House, Co. Kilkenny*

carriage with the children, though she was sometimes cautious about visiting because she and her sister-in-law Sarah were of very different temperaments. Sarah Tighe was impulsive and more emotional than Theodosia, who had learnt early in life to discipline her feelings. But Theodosia's children needed others to play with and soon Mary and John became close to the five young Tighes in the town house in Dominick Street in Dublin and during the summer months in the house and the gardens at Rossana where they could play safely after warnings about the brisk speed of the bubbling Vartry river at the foot of the lawns. Many years later in 1799 Mary would write a sonnet about her much-loved childhood playground:

> *Dear chestnut bower, I hail thy secret shade*
> *Image of tranquil life! Escaped yon throng,*
> *Who weave the dance, and swell the choral song,*
> *And all the summer's day have wanton played . . .*[1]

Sarah had dedicated herself to the care of her husband while he lived and according to her daughter Caroline, loved him dearly. She let her mother take over the upbringing of their eldest child.

> She idolised her husband and devoted herself to the care of her younger children. Her second son, Henry, was born six years after her marriage. Lady Betty [Fownes] had prevented her from nursing her eldest son William (born the first year) and had kept him at Woodstock, under the care of a nurse not notable for sobriety and my mother did not feel for him, during his childhood, the affection she felt for her other children. Her love for her husband was carried to such an excess that she could not bear him out of her sight. If she drove in her coach and four, with her little ones, he rode by her side, and though a person of first-rate abilities, he was governed by her, willingly – for he was passionately fond of her.[2]

Perhaps the clue to nature of Henry lies here in these early years spent at home as the favourite of a mother who cared less for her eldest son, an unusual situation. Safe from the threats posed by the eldest brother, who was settled comfortably at Woodstock with his grandparents, Henry was given the freedom to roam, the right to 'be himself', as recommended by the philosopher Jean-Jacques Rousseau, who spoke to intellectual young mothers such as Theodosia and Sarah with these words: 'It is to you that I address myself, tender and foresighted mother, who are capable of keeping the nascent shrub away from the highway and securing it from the impact of human opinions'.[3]

Some of Rousseau's practical advice had a fresh and modern simplicity which appealed to the new generation of women in the 1770s. He gave injunctions about mothering: she must breastfeed the child and bring it up on her own and not hand it over to a wet-nurse or governess; the baby should eat simple vegetarian food, such as working people eat, and lie unswaddled with freedom of limb and therefore expression. 'Bake for the teething child hard sticks of bread instead of handing out silver or coral teething rings' was his advice and 'bring him up close to nature'. The child must be educated in such a way as to make it self-reliant, confident and ready to cope with the problems the world would deliver.

In Book 1 of *Emile*, Rousseau seeks to reform the educational philosophy of his age:

> The children sent away or dispersed to boarding schools, convents, colleges will take the love belonging to the paternal home elsewhere, or, to put it better, they will bring back to the paternal home the habit of having no attachments. Brothers and sisters will hardly know one another. When all are gathered together for ceremonial occasions, they will be able to be quite polite with one another. They will treat one another as strangers.[4]

While Theodosia saw that Rousseau's admonitions required some sifting through and should only be acted upon with caution, Sarah leapt at them as justification for her own desires and decided to keep Henry at home as long as she could. In practice, Rousseau's freedoms seemed to do little for him as he was an unruly boy with a happy temperament but little desire to learn. He roamed free at Rossana for the first ten years of his life but seemed resistant to bookwork. His mother had not understood that, in his writing, Rousseau designates himself the all-seeing, worldly-wise mentor to the young Emile. Sarah herself could not provide a substitute for the tutor that Rousseau clearly sees himself to be.

Sarah Tighe's eldest boy William had already been sent to Eton, along with John Blachford. Harry was running wild and something had to be done. Both the boys were Mary's first cousins and their education was often discussed within the family. It was decided that, after all, Harry should go to boarding school and the days that seemed to the boy to be superlatively happy came to an end. Since 'some wise person remarked that brothers were generally better friends through life for having been educated at different schools', Harry was sent to Harrow. For an Irish child of the time, the journey was in itself an undertaking. He would travel by coach through County Wicklow to Dublin – some forty miles – take the ferry to Holyhead on his own or perhaps accompanied by a servant and then get a seat on the coach to London from where he set out west for Harrow. The very idea of this was too much for his mother, if not for her son and she decided that the whole family must move to live near him, despite the doubts of her husband, William Tighe, so Caroline writes:

> Henry was to be sent to Eton or Harrow, and my mother was peremptory in her resolution of accompanying him there. My father felt pain at the thought of becoming an absentee, contrary to his well known principles, and he was too sensible a man to believe that any good could result from a parent living with his son to watch over him at a public school where greater pains would probably be taken to corrupt him than if he had been left to himself from the spirit of opposition, so strong in schoolboys, but my mother was not accustomed to be contradicted and my father loved her too passionately not to yield to her wishes. They hired the best house they could get at Harrow which was the Vicarage close to the church yard, leaving Woodstock to spend its income on itself and its numerous dependants, and Rossana to the care of my father's brother, Richard, who was as remarkable for his justice, and accuracy, as for his kindness to the poor.[5]

The distress caused to William Tighe senior by the move to England was greater than his wife had anticipated. Loving as she was, Sarah acted on impulse and she had failed to think through the question of how the rest of the family would manage when the move to Harrow was in place. An only child herself and 'not accustomed to be contradicted', she found it difficult to think of the well-being of the whole family. Their life in England was in no way satisfying to her husband, who considered that it was the duty of every absentee to be liberal at home and frugal abroad. To be absent from his family estate, to evade in this way the duties to his tenants and to lose the lifelong friendship of his neighbours was a constant source of anxiety for William Tighe during the time at Harrow. He had doubts about the wisdom of his wife's upbringing of their second son, Harry, as well. Visits were made to London for Christmas and other festivities, and during the summer months the family sometimes returned only too briefly to Rossana, where the children enjoyed the freedom of the open spaces of the Wicklow countryside. Caroline writes: 'I remember the delight with which I used to run through the woods at Woodstock and play on the banks of the river at Rossana and with what regret we used to return to our small house at Harrow, its confined garden and green ponds.' Later in life, her elder brother William wrote of his childhood at Rossana:

> *Dear stream, how oft replenished by the rains*
> *Of winter, and by summer heats how oft*
> *Exhausted, have thy lively waters been,*
> *Since my first childhood on thy banks conceived*
> *Its early sports! To chase the dragonfly*
> *Led by his glittering mail and careless buzz;*
> *With vain attempt confine in fairy pools*
> *The eddying foam; or a mimic fall*
> *Of many-coloured pebbles guide its way...*[6]

The poem in which Wordsworth writes of his rural childhood in the Lake District, 'The Prelude', echoes in the work of William Tighe, who wrote these lines at about the same time. The two share a love of the countryside of their birth and an exhilarating joy in the natural world. Wordsworth's 'Prelude' was begun in 1798 and completed as a first draft in 1805. William published his poem 'The Plants' in 1808.

In the spring of 1782 the family returned to Dublin for a visit and the weather was bitterly cold. William Tighe the elder slipped and fell on the ice. He was sick for a week or so and then within a few days he died.

The 'uncommonly pleasing' father, so adored by his daughters, Caroline and Bess, and by his loving but impulsive wife, left a family bereft of his good influence. Sarah was only thirty-nine, still beautiful and possessed of a large income, the greatest part from an estate at her own disposal. She then determined to give up all her acquaintances, to devote herself exclusively to the education of her children, and to wear a widow's dress for the remainder of her life.

The whole family returned to Harrow and the Vicarage remained their base for the next six years. If Sarah Tighe had earlier hidden from her Irish obligations, she did so now to an even greater extent. Sublimating her grief in extravagant provision for her younger children, she supplied them with every kind of tutor – in music, languages, painting, drawing. William was safely at Eton, and he was perhaps fortunate to be away from his mother's influence at this stage. Harry was still the main focus of her attentions, and now even more so because his father had died. An assertive child, he dominated his mother's affections and she found it hard to turn down any of his suggestions. Caroline writes of this time with a despairing sense of loss for her father's good judgement. Sarah's 'fear of offending a set of ungovernable schoolboys had led her to do what she afterwards repented of having done'. And so:

> In order to please my brother [Harry] she allowed her house to be open to his friends. She feared lest he should consider her presence a troublesome restraint and was led to many things of which I am certain her judgement did not approve, but he was of an overbearing disposition and did as he pleased. She gave a feast to every boy he chose to invite every Sunday evening, sometimes she was persuaded to fit up the barn as a theatre for himself and his friends to act plays in. This may have encouraged a taste for the muses but not for morality, for nothing has ever proved more corrupting than a love of the stage, or so my father thought.[7]

It was the holidays and young William was back from Eton and ready to write a Prologue and Epilogue for *All the World's a Stage*. These were his first attempts at verse and many years later as he prepared to publish his volume of poetry, 'The Plants', he looked back at his first rhyming lines with amusement. Caroline remembers her younger brother, Harry, dressed up as a girl to play Kitty in *All the World's a Stage*. William certainly did not hold back in The Epilogue when he gives his younger brother the following words:

> *Perhaps good people, you may stare to see*
> *A boy duped up in petticoats like me,*
> *But hear my reasons and you'll cease to wonder.*
> *This is not ours but our strange age's blunder,*
> *For in the present age of contradiction,*
> *That woman rules the roost is not a fiction.*
> *Man has but one thing left him, which is*
> *The petticoat, for woman wears the breeches.*
> *Your modern wife her grandam will despise*
> *Poor vulgar soul that makes us shirts and pies!*
> *Her husband like her phaeton, she drives*
> *And yet the only thing untaxed are wives.*[8]

The play put on by the Tighe boys and their friends of a Sunday evening in their mother's house was judged by the headmaster of Harrow to be against the school rules of the time and he called upon Mrs Tighe to reprimand her. She strove to obey, but she continued to put on a weekly evening of entertainment when she tried to get the boys to talk about 'some useful subject', but they preferred a song and refreshments. Those refreshments were not just the simple offerings usually given to children. Sarah Tighe's stylish way of living never deserted her even in a crisis:

> The hot cakes and confectionary [sic] had arrived from London the night before by the carter, Nelly Bonsy, who is not long dead, and had carried packages backwards and forwards safely from London during half a century though roads at that time were infested with highwaymen. But the little woman in her covered cart passed unobserved.[9]

As her daughters grew during the family years at Harrow, Sarah Tighe turned her attention to how they should be educated. She and Theodosia met up in London where Mary was now attending school. Theodosia herself could speak several languages and took it for granted that her daughter should be taught to the same level. Sarah was not so sure. The family as a whole was very aware of the changes in women's education which had taken place over the last few generations. In her *Reminiscences,* William's sister Caroline writes of her maternal grandmother thus:

> My grandmother, though an Earl's daughter, could write only a short letter, containing a few short sentences in a very large hand, spelling very ignorantly and yet she was considered a sensible woman, and had energy enough to establish a little school at Inistioge, where girls were taught to make lace at a time when there were scarcely any schools for the poor in Ireland.[10]

Mary and Caroline could both write with fluency and accuracy at a very early age.

> Poor Lady Betty Fownes spent too much of her time working cross-stitch, as many sets of large chairs and carpets, now worn out, can testify – she lost her health by sitting almost the whole day at her work and died prematurely of debility before the age of sixty . . . Lady Betty must have had too some taste for literature if we may judge from her having left her name in many of the best authors of the day. She read, I have heard, well, and committed to memory many passages from Young and Milton while sitting at her work.[11]

Sarah Tighe was well educated and had much wider horizons than her mother. She brought up her children with 'modern' emphasis and Sarah's daughter Caroline became a gifted cartoonist and painter. Her work comments on the spirit of the age in a serious and critical manner that Lady Betty, as she bent over her cross-stitch, would have found hard to recognise as appropriate.

Mrs Sarah Tighe's arrangements for managing the Irish estates after the death of her husband were scanty. Income from Woodstock was 'spent on itself'; for example, on building an almshouse at Inistioge, with one school for Protestants and another for Catholics. Theodosia and Sarah discussed their respective financial situations and Theodosia pointed out the extravagant lifestyle that Sarah was adopting, warning her that soon she would be in debt. Many years later, her own daughter Caroline added her voice to the critics:

At Rossana too, clothes were distributed to the poor every Saturday and the tenants there met with equal liberality, but still my poor mother had no idea of limiting her own expenses in England. She had no taste for luxury or show, but she had no idea of economy and though her nominal income was £4,000 a year she began very soon to feel herself in debt.[12]

There were excursions to London to meet relations and to stay in the rented family house in Manchester Square with Theodosia, from where the two families made visits to Wesley's Chapel on City Road in London to take tea with the Methodists. A strong friendship developed with the Wesley brothers and both John and Charles would visit Rossana in later years and stay there to take a rest while touring the country. Theodosia was by nature devout and she encouraged Sarah to come along, believing that John Wesley would give good advice. Mary's cousin Caroline wrote:

> We visited Mr Wesley sometimes at his neat house adjoining the chapel at Moorfields, and I felt the greatest admiration for him. I recollect his custom of awakening the attention of his hearers by some familiar anecdote not easily forgotten. Mr Wesley's authoritative yet persuasive manner made a great impression upon the lower classes of society, as did also his itinerant preachers, who mixed familiarly with them, always endeavouring to give their conversation a religious tone.[13]

Mary Blachford had finished her formal education and there was no question of her continuing to study, but the question that now preoccupied the family was where Harry should go to university. Sarah wrote to her sister-in-law to solicit her opinion and Theodosia Blachford replied that she had considered the very same matter as regards her own son John and with an uncharacteristic flash of anger and lack of moderation she said, 'I should as soon send him to hell as to Cambridge'. She went on:

> His father was very exemplary in his attention to his studies, of which his sitting twice for a scholarship was indisputable proof, and he had no father to check or stimulate him, no more than John has, for his father died the very first year of his admission. Indeed many times I have heard him bless God for living at home with his mother, the two first years of his being in the University . . .[14]

There was no room for debate here, and as Theodosia continues her comments on her nephew Harry's university education, her common sense and awareness of their Irish identity shines through her writing. What, she enquires, did Sarah Tighe think she would gain by sending her son to be educated in England?

> . . . he might acquire more learning and more polished manners at Oxford or Cambridge than in Dublin, but if idle and profligate, he may find more temptations to extravagance and idleness there meeting with so many gentlemanlike associates of a superior description to himself, calculated to make him despise his home and his Irish friends. Even well conducted men have been made lovers of England rather than lovers of learning by being educated there. All our most distinguished lawyers, Pennyfeathers, Plunket, Warren, etc etc with all our most eloquent and learned Divines of the present day were educated at Dublin College [Trinity]. They never questioned its learning or its respectability and lived with their parents and friends, who were freed from anxiety on their account by seeing them occupied with their studies in their own happy homes and many a father and mother's heart has leapt for joy when the quick loud knock at the hall door after the examinations seemed to be the forerunner of the good news that their son has got a premium.[15]

The good sense and honesty of Theodosia illuminate her words and probably she did sway Sarah Tighe, for Harry went to Trinity College, Dublin. But Caroline's comments on her brother had now become tart:

> . . . a boy without a father to guide or control him, and with an indulgent mother too timid to oppose his inclinations openly is always in a dangerous situation, wherever he may be placed. It was under such circumstances that my brother entered Dublin College.[16]

The Tighe family returned to live permanently at Rossana where Sarah Tighe kept a comfortable, lively house offering extravagant hospitality which she could not afford. Caroline resisted many of the efforts by her mother to 'improve' her, but decided that drawing was a subject that she liked. In 1788, Sarah Tighe invited Jonathan Spilsbury, who had been Art Master at Harrow and was already a well-established portrait painter, to come to live in Ireland to give the girls drawing lessons. Jonathan and his wife Rebecca accepted. Mrs Spilsbury was an accomplished pianist and would teach the children to play. They planned to go for just a few weeks but stayed for nearly a year, one in which their daughter flourished and grew plump and spent much time playing outside with the Tighe and Blachford children. Of the Moravian faith, the Spilsburys felt a kinship with Sarah Tighe and Theodosia Blachford, who were both Methodists, and their daughter Rebecca Maria joined in lessons with Elizabeth and Caroline. Mr Spilsbury had them practise techniques of all kinds and observe the great masters. This training would bear fruit, for both Rebecca Maria Spilsbury (to be known after her marriage as Maria Spilsbury Taylor) and Caroline Tighe became accomplished artists. When Caroline was older, she chose Hogarth and Rowlandson for her models, as her satirical paintings testify. She comments on the social ills of her time and in a drawing entitled *Domestic Happiness as acted in this city, a tragic-comic farce* below, a liveried servant offers three thin children a bone on a silver salver while to the right a fashionable woman in the wide skirts of the period hides under her dress a plate of rich food at which a dog sniffs appreciatively.

*Caroline Hamilton's satirical comment on the double standards of the age. Children are offered a bare bone while an elegant mother hides ample provisions under her skirt.*

Like her cousin Mary, Caroline had looked into the eyes of begging children and in her satirical painting attempts to draw attention to their plight. The friendship between Caroline and Mr Spilsbury's daughter flourished. Rebecca Maria would much later return to Ireland and paint John Wesley preaching under a tree at Rossana. She was by then married to John Taylor. Her brief encounter with the Tighe family had a lasting effect: perhaps the child-centred culture of her parents' church and their interest in Rousseau, shared with the Tighes, gave her confidence and the liberty to be herself, which encouraged her artistic nature to develop.

*Mary's cousin, Caroline Hamilton, painter and diarist, c.1797*

Many guests were welcomed at Rossana, including young Mary Blachford, fresh out of school and about to launch herself in Dublin society, despite her mother's wishes. She played the harp and there were many musical sessions about the house and particularly in the Long Room. Caroline felt sorry for Mary, obliged as she was always to listen to Theodosia's disapproving remarks, and she observed that her cousin was starting to veer towards wanting to join the family at Rossana. John was away and Mary was lonely and lacking in confidence. However, Caroline herself was due to go abroad:

> It was soon after this that, as my brother had finished his studies at Harrow, my mother conceived the plan of joining my eldest brother [William] abroad for the purpose of going to Italy with all her children for a year.[17]

Caroline Tighe was just ten years old and when her mother wanted her confirmed with her brother Henry before the journey to Italy, Bishop Porteous objected, saying that the girl was very young for confirmation. Caroline never forgot the look he gave her, shaking his head as much as to say Italy was a bad place for a young family. Theodosia Blachford was deeply disapproving of Sarah's extraordinary continental travelling nursery – there was no chance that her daughter Mary would be allowed to join her cousins. Indeed Sarah Tighe herself became so anxious about the adventure that a lock of her hair turned grey overnight. She did not abandon the plan to join William, however, though the journey was curtailed and Italy removed from the itinerary, which included France, Flanders and Holland. So Henry left Harrow and the family departed to meet up with William in Paris where, Caroline says of Bess:

> My sister, a little older than I was, went to see Louis XVIth and his family at dinner. That unfortunate monarch, endeavouring to gain popularity, allowed everyone who pleased to see him and his family eating their dinner on particular days, separated from them by a railing only. And it was thought great amusement to see him tearing a chicken asunder and picking its bones as he was often seen to do.[18]

Caroline was not so lucky and was given a less interesting task. She was sent to a convent to deliver a message from the pious Theodosia about Madame de Chantal whose works her aunt had translated. The journey itself was by no means easy and included Susan Butticuz, adopted into the family, daughter of a Harrow schoolmaster:

> We travelled through a part of France, Flanders and Holland, moving in such a cavalcade as is seldom now seen with commoners. First went my brother [William] in his chaise and four, my sister and I going with him occasionally – his courier, with heavy boots, riding after us cracking his whip. I was very happy when it was my turn to be his little companion, for my mother's coach and four was filled with dogs and children, my brother John not always manageable and Susan Butticuz not always good-humoured. Another coach followed with two maids and a Swiss man and our luggage, consisting of portfolios, books, sheets, etc.[19]

Apart from a tumble 'in one of the most swampy parts of the Netherlands' when the carriage overturned and the family was held up for a few days by a maid who had broken her collarbone, there were no serious mishaps, except for a tendency of the locals to swindle them. It is significant that Sarah would not continue without her maid: 'My mother never abandoned her servants when they were in distress'.

The modern observer may, like Mary Blachford, view this expedition to the Continent more favourably than Theodosia and even consider it to have been of educational benefit. Sarah claimed that she had hoped to expand her family's horizons, but all good things must end and the party divided after Holland, William returning to Paris and the rest of the family to Rossana where they regaled Mary with all they had seen, which served both to entertain her and also to set alight a little flame of rebellion which would soon kindle to something more dangerous: a determination to do the opposite of what her mother recommended.

NOTES

1  Sonnet: 'Written at Rossana', 1799.
2  Caroline Hamilton: *Reminiscences*, NLI 4811.
3  Jean-Jacques Rousseau: *Emile,* or *On Education*, 1762.
4  ibid.
5  Caroline Hamilton: *Reminiscences*, NLI 4811.
6  William Tighe: *The Plants*, London, 1808.
7  Caroline Hamilton: *Reminiscences*, NLI 4811.
8  William Tighe: Epilogue written for *All the World's a Stage*, NLI 4811.
9  Caroline Hamilton: *Reminiscences*, NLI 4811.
10  ibid.
11  ibid.
12  ibid.
13  ibid.
14  Letter: Theodosia Blachford to Sarah Tighe, 1788, PRONI.
15  ibid.
16  Caroline Hamilton: *Reminiscences*, NLI 8411.
17  ibid.
18  ibid.
19  ibid.

# CHAPTER 3

# SOCIAL LIFE IN DUBLIN
## *'In busy idleness'*

Despite the move to Harrow, the childhood of the Tighe boys was relatively secure compared to that of their cousin Mary Blachford, whose way of life was peripatetic since she had no real home of her own after the early years at the four-towered castle in County Wicklow. John Blachford and his young family would not return to Altidore until 1807. This pattern was to some extent the norm for Anglo-Irish families, but the Tighes moved often and there is no doubt but that this affected Mary's development. Theodosia took her children to Dublin to the Tighe house in Dominick Street and to another in Gardiner Row. They went for a while to London to live in Manchester Square and Mary started some schooling at Mrs Esté's educational establishment. Since brother John was at Eton, this fitted in nicely. And then they went back to Ireland for the holidays and down to Rossana. The pattern of restless travel persists into Mary's maturity after her marriage, her mother often in tow, keeping an eye on her daughter's consumptive cough.

The period of the late 1780s was a fine time for the young and sociable who liked to come up to balls in the centre of Dublin. The age of the fortification of the castle was over and much rebuilding took place at Dublin Castle in the eighteenth century. The state rooms and reception areas dominated the building and their grand and spacious style was in keeping with the character of the new areas of Dublin which were being developed. In 1787 the Wide Street Commission, an agency set up by

Act of Parliament in 1757, was given extensive powers compulsorily to purchase property. North of the Liffey the fine houses of Henrietta Street and Dominick Street were speedily constructed and faced each other across pleasant, spacious roads. St Stephen's Green, Fitzwilliam and Merrion Squares were built to the new scale and everywhere a mood of prosperity bloomed. Building continued on the Irish Parliament – now The Bank of Ireland – which stands at the foot of Dame Street and faces Trinity College, the superlative grandeur of style a statement of Ireland's belief in her ability to resolve her own problems.

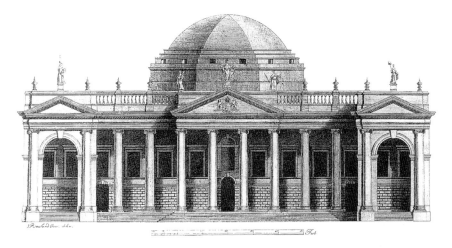

*Elevation of Parliament House, Dublin, by Peter Mazell*

In the 1780s, at about fourteen, Mary Blachford was first launched into Dublin society by Sarah Tighe of Rossana, home for the holidays from Harrow, who described her niece as 'a great beauty…and much admired'[1]. Not only was she attractive, as her aunt claimed, she was also sensitive, poised and highly intelligent, though unwilling to allow this last characteristic to be revealed to the public. The streets were too dirty and dangerous for walking, so she was driven by her aunt to balls at the Castle. They joined the queue of elegant carriages that filled Dame Street from top to bottom and the carriage would jostle along a few paces every few minutes until it was their turn to drive into the Upper Castle Yard where passengers would alight. Those arriving by sedan chair might park their vehicles in the open arcades while they attended the functions of the viceregal court. Mary Blachford had the satisfaction of seeing the tower of St Werburgh's church loom up over the castle wall; it was here that her grandfather had been rector and her father buried. Guests ascended the graceful staircase to the Battleaxe Landing and went on up to the Drawing Room where young ladies waited with their chaperones to be asked to dance in St Patrick's Hall, checking in the floor-level mirrors that the hems of their petticoats were not showing beneath their dresses. To reach the Hall, they had to go through the Throne Room where the canopy with crown, lion and unicorn had just been erected over the seat of the Viceroy, who received his guests there. After the dance, the men returned the young ladies to their chaperones in the Drawing Room where they had to sit in hope that another invitation would be offered. Mary had plenty. She danced with young Ascendancy sons, with soldiers on duty at the Castle and with her cousin William. Henry Tighe was still at Harrow. Much to her relief, here there were no keen young Methodists for her mother to push forward as suitors.

*The Great Courtyard, Dublin Castle 1792 by James Malton,*
*St Werburgh's church tower in the background*

The Castle at the top of Dame Street was in fact a symbolically fortified retreat for the Ascendancy, the Anglo-Irish rulers of Ireland. The main task of the Viceroy who lived so comfortably at Dublin Castle was to ensure that the English monarch retained governance over the Irish – and this had been the case since the defeat of James by William of Orange at the Battle of the Boyne in 1690. The entertainment offered at this viceregal court had always been lavish, especially as regards the tradition of looking after the social welfare of the Anglo-Irish elite who came into town from their mansions in rural Ireland or from their town houses in ever-expanding Dublin. The last three decades of this, the eighteenth century, were the most remarkable of all times in the history of the social events at the Castle: it was as if the extravagance was a kind of fiendish bubble which must burst: the tension was tangible.

About this time, a young aide-de-camp, newly commissioned to the army, took up his post at Dublin Castle. This young man had come from London where his mother had helped him prepare for this new stage of his life. He had left Eton very early to make way for his academically brighter younger brothers, and so far his only training was in horse-riding: he had attended a course at Angers in France, and learnt not only to ride, but also to speak French well. He was nineteen when he arrived in Dublin in 1788. His name was Arthur Wellesley, one day to be the Duke of Wellington. But he was as yet the ugly duckling of the family in his mother's eyes. The third son of the Wellesley family, he suffered not only from his lowly position among his siblings, but also from the fact that his father Garret had died in 1781 when Arthur was only twelve. Garret Wellesley was very musical, and Arthur inherited his love of music and his skill in performance. Brought up for the early part of his life at Dangan in County Meath, he was very much part of the Anglo-Irish circle of families who intermarried over the many years they lived in Ireland and held the reins of power: Plunkets, Fitzgeralds, Cusacks, Colleys and Wesleys, or Wellesley, as they now preferred to be called, had intermarried for centuries. The Tighes and Wellesleys were known to each other both through the political activities of the families in Dublin and the social events at the Castle where Mary and Arthur met. Later on in her life, much later, when he was a great deal more than the third son of the family and she was a sick woman dying of consumption, he would visit her at her family house in Dominick Street, calling with many others to cheer her final days.

However, there was another side entirely to this life in society where each day was given to considering which dress to wear. Mary Blachford was growing up in a world that reacted strongly to the excesses of the courtly life at the Castle and the extravagantly showy style of dressing. At about this time Theodosia started a charitable foundation for poor women in the centre of Dublin on Baggot Street, which would later become the House of Refuge. She was now a committed Methodist and made her own protest against the sybaritic indulgence of the Dublin socialites by embracing the simple life of her faith. It is impossible to imagine Theodosia going to a social event in a sedan chair with a cupola specially raised to accommodate a three-foot hairpiece, as did many of the Ascendancy ladies of the day. Nor would she have been prepared to sit at a table on which thirty to forty different types of dish were served together with fifteen bowls of sweetmeats standing on a separate trestle throughout the meal. Her daughter was torn between the more liberal attitudes of her aunt, Sarah Tighe, and the passionately held non-conformist views of her mother with which she had been inculcated from an early age.

As Mary journeyed in her carriage, she observed the remarkable disparity of wealth in this country that she called her own. The Irish Catholics who worked on the estates of the great houses that she visited were subject to penal restrictions and occupied a subservient role. They were deeply impoverished and, while in the countryside the suffering was evident, it was not as blatant as the city poverty which Mary saw daily in Dublin, where the poorer areas jostled next to the new streets that were being built and the indigent begged at the windows of the carriages of the wealthy. She did not know whether to give what little she could afford or to turn her head away. Her journey was always completed safely but Mary carried in her mind the scenes she observed

– tiny, scrawny babies, emaciated beggars and skinny, ragged children who stared her in the eye: the after-images would not disappear. Her aunt said to think of other things, while Theodosia, pragmatic as ever, turned to her charitable works.

Less practical than her mother, Mary picked up her pen to write. She had been encouraged to keep a spiritual journal, as was common practice amongst the devout at this time. From the age of fourteen she often wrote her diary and some, though not much of it, survives, the main body of writing having been deemed unacceptable by a later expurgating hand, probably Theodosia's. The modern reader senses the strains imposed upon the young woman by her mother's wish for her and perceives a strong rebellion against parental authority. She returns again and again to the battle within her soul. Given the contrast between the merry times spent as a young debutante at the ball and the serious, devotional life that Theodosia wished her daughter to lead, it is easy to see why Mary Blachford felt considerable tension. The opening lines of the extant journal reflect this theme:

> When I look back and consider my past life (short as it has been) I see in it such an astonishing medley it causes me at times not to know what to think. Some part of my life I have been immersed in sin, and if I may say in the very jaws of the wicked one and others rejoicing in the belief that I was in the favour of God and certainly whether I was in that deceived or not it was the happiest part of my life. At other periods I have been in a state which I cannot otherwise describe than by saying I was asleep.[2]

In the following entry, dated May 1789 and written at the family house in Dublin in Gardiner's Row, she writes of life at her Aunt Sarah Tighe's house at Rossana in a manner that may well reflect her mother's tone:

> Low-spirited, perhaps, at leaving Rossana. If I have not philosophy enough to despise or at least to disregard the gaiety which reigns there, which inclines everyone to eat drink and to rise up to play and to make the pleasures of the present moment their waking passions, I have at least sense to despise myself. Yet I am afraid that it is that the gay scene has seduced my heart that I lament its absence.[3]

The journal reflects the dilemmas of Mary's conscience:

> Sometimes my heart has been distracted by vain pleasures. False hopes, foolish disappointments, idle pursuits – trifling sorrows, useless alarms and childish vexations. Alas! My thoughts are more intent upon worldly knowledge, worldly fame and worldly pleasures than upon that knowledge which can alone be useful to my immortal soul. (Saturday 21 August 1790)[4]

Life at the Castle continued unabated: particular feasts were designated 'largesse feasts' and the Governor would allow the public to take away what was left of the meals. When the herald proclaimed at the doors 'largesse, largesse, largesse', the poor were let in and women of the town rushed into the room and waited for food to be passed by the guests to them. Dressed in rags, dirty in a way that only townspeople can be, they brought with them a sense of misrule. Sometimes disorder broke out and they grabbed food from the table under the noses of guests. 'I am tired of Dublin and all its claret ... swarming with poverty and idleness,[5]' wrote Henry Grattan, the parliamentarian. Indeed, a generation earlier Mrs Delany, more famed for her artistic merits than her political acumen, had warned of the dangers of over-indulgence:

> I don't find that the troubles of the times have given any check to gay doings in this part of the world. The castle is crowded twice a week; plays, assembly and drums are as much frequented as ever. I must own this may be a right policy to keep up the hopes of people, but I am surprised that their spirits should hold out; and I cannot but think, under the terrible apprehensions of losing our liberty and our property, it would be more becoming to abate our diversions, especially as we have reason to think that the great irreligion and luxury of the times have brought our present calamities on us. (21 December 1745)[6]

And Lord Nuneham, writing when his father, Simon, 1st Earl of Harcourt, was Lord Lieutenant, said of his visit to Dublin:

> This is the most dirty, the most gloomy, the most stinking and the ugliest city I was ever in ... every kind of filth is thrown into the deep stream of black mud that gently flows through the town ... half the inhabitants are in absolute rags and some of them ... almost naked. You cannot stop in a carriage without being surrounded with crowds of importunate beggars.[7]

Theodosia was certainly not being over-protective when she expressed her concern about the number and frequency of Mary's visits to the Castle:

> She was scarcely fourteen when she awakened my solicitude by being noticed by daring and artful young men every way her inferiors and though her openness with me prevented any very serious apprehensions on the subject, yet it made me very prematurely anxious to see her well disposed of.[8]

Just a few years later, Mary was able to see clearly what had happened to her when she realised that the 'circles of the vain and gay' had led her to a life dominated by 'mirth and dress and song':

> *For in the circles of the vain and gay,*
> *No more her tranquil state my soul enjoyed,*
> *In busy idleness I passed the day,*
> *And mirth and dress and song my hours employed.*[9]

But for the time being, she suspended her conscience and enjoyed herself. Indeed, her cousin Caroline uses the word 'coquetting' to describe her behaviour. She went on to say:

> It was her idea that learning and talents in women never excited love and while young, she was willing to pass for having neither. I remember hearing it remarked that Mary Tighe was very pretty but had not much sense: indeed she often chose for her companions those who were very far below the rest of her world in talents, if they loved her. She never tried to shine in conversation and was often considered too silent in company.[10]

Theodosia thought it was time to act and she arranged introductions for her daughter to young religious men, hoping that she would thus be brought into the fold and the temptations of the whirl of Ascendancy social life removed for ever by a happy marriage close to the family. The first young man to be thus promoted was William Myles, born in 1756 and sixteen years older than Mary. He was a Methodist who had been converted by John Wesley on one of his many visits to Ireland and from 1777 to 1782 he was an itinerant preacher. It seems he did take an interest in Mary Blachford, though hardly a serious one. The next to be brought to the attention of Theodosia and then of Mary was Mr de la Flechière, the nephew of Revd John Fletcher. Theodosia later admitted that in fact she herself wished that the relationship would be successful and it becomes clear that she simply picked de la Flechière as a suitably pious young man for her daughter to marry without reflecting upon Mary's own wishes. He is described in Caroline Hamilton's journal thus:

> …young M. de la Flechière came from Switzerland to visit his Uncle – he was considered a religiously disposed young man, and his aunt, Mrs Fletcher, sent him to Dublin to visit the little circle of his friends there, chiefly Methodists, among whom Mrs Blachford, from her rank in society, was a prominent person, the Methodists at that time being in general, people in humbler life. Mrs Blachford's interesting daughter was attractive to the uncle and aunt.[11]

Theodosia had to struggle with the realisation that she had in her daughter not simply a miniature version of herself. This young woman did not want to marry a burgeoning Methodist whose uncle had been one of the founder members of the group of clergymen who came to Ireland in the early days of the movement. Theodosia nevertheless pressed her case:

> Her [Mary's] reflections on this subject, in her journal, are natural, innocent and just – In the course of this year I embraced with unaccountable warmth the prospect of her marrying Monr. de la Flechière (nephew to Mr. Flechière of Madeley) . . . My heart became so set upon this match that I do not think any temporal disappointment, except her not having children, and similar circumstance, ever gave me so much pain at its not being accomplished.[12]

It was left to Theodosia to write the last letter to young de la Flechière about the demise of the relationship. Her daughter was seventeen. Theodosia was torn between the gratification to be found in society's approval of her offsprings' characters and fear that they would be led astray from the spiritual life in which she had endeavoured to rear them. The workings of her children's hearts were in crucial ways unknown to her and out of her control.

William had emerged from Eton and Cambridge, just as his own father had done. He was five years older than his brother Harry and so had benefited longer from the presence of his capable and accomplished father before his early death in 1782 when William was sixteen. He had been brought up by his grandparents at Woodstock House and, as the eldest child, had escaped some of his mother's later, more daring experiments with Rousseau's advice on how to raise children. He saw himself as heir to Woodstock, the grand and prosperous estate that came into the Tighe family through his mother. He was, as well, heir to Rossana, his father's estate. Two years after his father's death William was admitted to St John's College, Cambridge as a Fellow-Commoner, the same college at which his father had studied before him. He suffered none of his brother Harry's reluctance to learn. During his time at Cambridge he became MP for Banagher, Co. Offaly (then King's County) a seat he held until 1797, though he was not yet active in Irish politics, but would become so in his maturity. In terms of accomplishments and inheritance, he was every inch fit to woo his cousin Mary Blachford. Marriages between first cousins were then considered acceptable, securing as they did land and wealth within the family.

There is no doubt that the younger boy Harry had a tendency to see himself as the rival of his accomplished and well-schooled older brother. Despite all the imaginative resources of his early education, despite his carefree early childhood at home at Rossana under the eye of his parents and his time at Harrow closely supervised by his mother, Harry ended his school years with very little by way of knowledge that he could usefully use in the wider world. He seemed temperamentally inclined to pursue a life of pleasure. And he was undoubtedly very charming. Harry's envy of his older brother who stood to inherit so much (and he so little) took the form of a refusal to conform to the Tighe blueprint of a successful young man in terms of achievement.

In a letter to her older son, 'My dear Billy', dated 26 May 1788, Sarah Tighe tries to enlist William's help. Harry would like to travel abroad like his older brother, but Sarah is more concerned about the pressing matter of Harry's education:

> If you could persuade him of the necessity of being grounded in the rudiments of science, particularly mathematics, before he goes to a University, possibly he might take Euclid in his pocket, and would certainly find in every great town some learned Abbé to assist him in his studies.[13]

*William Tighe (1766-1816) by George Romney*

Sarah's idea that Harry, the reluctant learner, might be ready to seek out and ask the advice of a cleric about his mathematics homework in each city he visited abroad while travelling on the Grand Tour is touchingly naive. Her parenting was always enthusiastic but often out of tune with the real characters of her children and the world in which they lived.

Now that Mary was in her teens, her cousins were suddenly both drawn to her. She had become a beautiful young woman when they were not looking; the infant cousin, the long-legged girl who hung round their games, had become a personality in her own right, highly intelligent and well read, yet with a sense of fun and a capacity to enjoy herself that was sometimes irresistible. It was William who first became aware of Mary as a person in her early teens, while she saw him as sensible rather than sensitive in the fashionable manner. But she was too young to respond, too uncertain of what she

*Sarah Tighe, copy of portrait by Maria Spilsbury Taylor*

herself wanted from life. She just took him for granted, a kind of elder brother who had always been there. Yet she felt most confident dancing with William and she learnt from him how to move joyfully round the great ballroom at The Castle. There was no effort required to be partnered by him, all seemed simple. A certain closeness could be expected and accepted. But she felt unready to make so grand a decision as to whom she might marry. She hesitated. And William was aware already of his cousin's disturbing cough which from time to time troubled her. Was she right for him? Could she bear him the family he knew he one day desired to have? It was too soon to decide. Mary was younger; she would mature and see things differently perhaps. And soon he was saying with all the bravado of the young traveller determined to leave: 'The sea is much easier passed than the mountains of Wicklow and mankind are exactly the same everywhere.'[14]

Sarah had little skill in approaching such subjects tactfully and her insistent reminders that William should marry and take on the responsibilities of the family estates may well have persuaded her elder son to react in just the manner she feared. His lengthy Grand Tour began in 1788 and continued until 1792, nearly four years. He went far and wrote sometimes furiously to the mother who had called him a 'criminal' in need of salvation, as in the following letter:

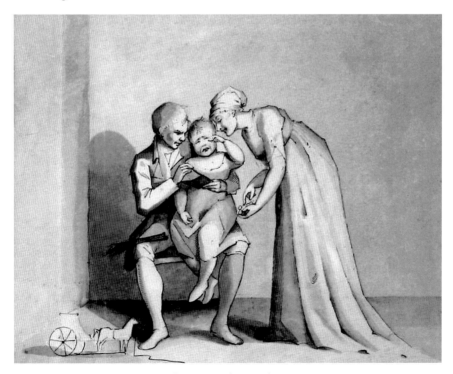

*Caroline Hamilton: Education.*
*Parents pore over their child, who does not seem to be happy.*

May you also be brought like a repentant criminal to the rock of your salvation. I hope you marry soon – one worthy of you. I shall be more at ease about you when you are married and settled down at Woodstock. May you meet with one as good and simple and devoted to God as my Bess.[15]

But William was to discover that mankind was not just the same everywhere and that the heart does not recover from life's early impressions as easily as one might hope. And into the gap he left at home stepped his younger brother, Harry, who had perhaps been waiting for just this moment since his infancy.

NOTES

1 Letter from Sarah Tighe to Theodosia Blachford, PRONI 2685/1/34.
2 *Journal of Mary Tighe*: NLI 4810.
3 ibid.
4 ibid.
5 *Memoirs of the Life and Times of Henry Grattan*, London, 1839.
6 *The Autobiography and Correspondence of Mary Granville, Mrs Delany*: Richard Bentley, London, 1861.
7 *Memoirs of the Life and Times of Henry Grattan* by his Son, London, 1839.
8 Theodosia Blachford: *Observations on the Journal of Mary Tighe*, NLI 4810.
9 'Verses Written in Solitude', April 1792.
10 Caroline Hamilton: *Mary Tighe*, NLI 4810.
11 Caroline Hamilton: *Mary Tighe*, NLI 4810.
12 Theodosia Blachford: *Observations on the Journal of Mary Tighe*, NLI 4810.
13 Letter from Sarah Tighe to William Tighe, 1788, PRONI 2685.
14 Letter from William Tighe to Sarah Tighe, 1788, PRONI 2685.
15 Letter from Sarah Tighe to William Tighe, 1788, PRONI 2685.

# CHAPTER 4

# VENTURING INTO THE WORLD
## *'The frail bark'*

Mary Blachford had the skills of a courtier and several suitors but none that had claimed her heart. One of her admirers had taken the significant step of leaving his anxious mother to manage the family estates and had set out on the Grand Tour on a series of journeys which were far less glamorous than their title suggests, contemporary modes of travel being anything but luxurious. But every young man of any strength of mind would wish to make the Grand Tour to complete his education and to gain much-needed experience of the world. William responded furiously to his mother's nagging letters, which told him all her financial problems, her worries about his safety and quite frequently of her ill-health. And Mary's persistent cough was beginning to give cause for concern. None of these things did William want to hear about, except perhaps the news of Mary. His tour lasted from 1788–1792. He travelled to Paris, Rome, Orléans, Vienna, Budapest, Warsaw, St Petersburg, Stockholm, Berlin and Dresden, covering distances much greater than the average young man of his day. His perseverance and resilience were honed on long journeys in unsprung carriages across many kilometres of French, German, Austrian and Polish unmade roads and on the watch on board ship in the Baltic during 'a fresh gale'; and it was these same qualities that would one day much later in their lives bring him back to be Mary's caring guardian. And in 1791 as William Tighe still travelled across Europe and to Russia, Mary Blachford wrote her first sonnet in simple rhyming couplets:

> *As the frail bark, long tossed by stormy winds,*
> *Weary and scattered a calm haven finds,*
> *So from a heavy load of cares set free,*
> *At length, O Lord! My soul returns to thee!*[1]

Her chosen simile of 'the frail bark' is a very apt one for this moment in her life. Mary felt herself to be fragile; she had little security. The standards of the day were such that the question of finding a suitor was a priority not only for Mary herself but also for those close to her, and it was not until later in her life that she would come to question her passive acceptance of the convention. There is no doubt but that this subject was always on her mind, as was the now vexed matter of religion. The pages that remain of her spiritual journal reflect a continuing desire to live the pious, intellectual life to which she saw her mother was dedicated, and yet simultaneously her words tell of a deep-seated wish to be free. Theodosia's influence was powerful and she had friends in significant places. When John Wesley came to Ireland during this period, he stayed several times at Rossana and visited the Tighes and Blachfords in Dublin. Mary welcomed him with enthusiasm but she found in her relations with him exactly the same dilemmas that she faced with her mother:

11 April 1789

Mr Wesley breakfasted with us in Gardiner's [*sic*] Row. I sat next to him. After breakfast he prayed, remembering me in the most tender and ardent manner. When he rose from his knees he took hold of my hand and said 'dear Molly, expect that there are blessings in store for you', he turned to my bookcase and said 'there are many books here, Molly, not worth your reading', and then observed a good deal on idle books, particularly fine poetry. Said that History and religious books were the best study. Praised French Historians and condemned Hume and the Abbé Raynal as an enemy to all power human and divine – he spoke about the beggars not in such harsh terms as I have heard even those who are accounted pious persons express themselves. His words were all tenderness and compassion.[2]

John Wesley was a man of extraordinary energy and understanding and Mary sensed his great wish for her in religious matters. She had heard many times of his conversion, of the experience of being 'plucked like a brand from the burning'[3]. He told her how he and his brother had started the first Methodist Society in London in The Foundry near Moorfields, a disused cannon factory that was to remain their London headquarters for almost forty years. This building could hold 1,500 people in congregation, and there was room for a small school and places to store the books that Wesley published and sold. He told her how he had decided that there would be no grand dining area in his home but that all his household servants would eat at the same table as himself. The significance of this democratic gesture touched Mary to the quick. She thought of the hedonistic extravagance of the Castle banquets at which she herself had dined and longed to be at John Wesley's simple board.

He travelled farther afield each year, preaching in towns and villages, most often in the open air. The Methodists had gained a strong following and the Wesleys felt the need for larger premises in London: they started to raise money for the Chapel which stands today on City Road in London. After the opening in 1778, Wesley moved into the house next door and lived there until his death in 1791. The tall, simple building survives as it was when Theodosia Blachford and her daughter Mary visited it on their many trips to London in the 1780s. They worshipped at the chapel and afterwards took tea with Wesley in his home. An early riser, and a man who went early to bed, every day of his long life was used energetically in the name of his faith and he insisted those around him did the same. He wrote a diary (in shorthand, which is economical of time and paper) where the events of each well-used day were recorded. As early as 1752 he travelled to Ireland and began the formidable task of converting the Irish, Protestants and Papists alike. With his characteristic simplicity of thinking, Wesley described what he considered to be the solution to the root of the problem:

> There is one way, and one way only, one that will infallibly succeed. If this way is taken, I am willing to stake my life upon the success of it. And it is a plain simple way, such as may be taken by any man, though but of a small capacity. For it requires no depth of understanding, no extraordinary

height of learning; but only a share of common sense, and an honest, upright heart. Here, therefore, is the short and sure method. Let all the clergy of the Church of Ireland only *live* like the apostles, and *preach* like the apostles, and the thing is done.[4]

He did not fully know, as yet, the clergy of the Church of Ireland and he was to be disillusioned when he did. He was nonetheless still determined, and it was this determination that so affected others. Theodosia and Sarah in their own ways tried to be virtuous and energetic Methodists and for the large part succeeded. John Wesley's simplicity and restraint impressed Mary Blachford at a time when so much was profligate.

Wesley seemed to be able to think positively despite negative experiences: 'For natural sweetness of temper, for courtesy and hospitality, I have never seen any people like the Irish'. In the early days of his mission, the work was always tough, sometimes dangerous, as is evidenced by this incident in Kilkenny described in his journal for 11 July 1762:

> I went to the cathedral, one of the best built that I have ever seen in Ireland. At six in the evening, I began preaching on the old bowling green near the castle. Abundance of people, Protestants and Papists, gathered from all parts. They were very still during the former part of the sermon; then the Papists ran together, set up a shout, and would have gone further, but they were restrained, they knew not how. I turned to them and said, 'Be silent, or be gone!' Their noise ceased and we heard them no more; so I resumed and went on with my discourse and concluded without interruption.
>
> When I came out of the green they gathered again and gnashed upon me with their teeth; one cried out, 'Och! What is Kilkenny come to?' But they could go no further. Only two or three large stones were thrown; but none was hurt save he that threw them, for, as he was going to throw again, one seized him by the neck and gave him a kick or a cuff which spoiled his diversion.[5]

By June 1789, Wesley takes a more relaxed attitude, resting on a sense of achievement, and his diary entry reads: 'I went on to Mrs Tighe's at Rossana, near Wicklow, an exceeding pleasant seat, deeply embosomed in woods on every side. In the evening I preached in the great hall, to about one hundred very genteel persons. I believe most of them felt as well as heard; some, perhaps, may bring forth fruit.'[6] This was in fact Wesley's last visit to Ireland. He had stayed several times at Rossana at the invitation of Sarah Tighe, who was less austere in her faith than Theodosia Blachford but nonetheless devoted to him. In 1789 Wesley also stayed in Drumballyroney as the guest of Theodosia's half-brother, Thomas, the Methodist vicar who helped a young local student, Patrick Brunty, soon to become Brontë, with Latin and Greek; Brontë was to go to St John's, Cambridge, the Tighe brothers' college. St John's College had strong Methodist affiliations as well as a reputation for willingness to help poor students who had a sponsor to recommend them.

*The drawing room at Rossana painted by Maria Spilsbury Taylor. Here John Wesley preached and his brother Charles composed hymns.*

It was Sarah, the manager of this busy household, who arranged for the now famous portrait of Wesley to be painted by George Romney, who, unlike Sir Joshua Reynolds, was a man from a working-class background and one with whom Wesley was inclined to be patient and admiring of his achievement. He was, Wesley said, a painter who worked faster than Sir Joshua – and time was of the essence. At a later date Maria Spilsbury Taylor, whose father was employed by Sarah Tighe to teach her daughters, returned to Ireland to live as a married woman with her family.

*John Wesley preaching under a tree in Ireland: Maria Spilsbury Taylor*

She used a copy of Romney's portrait for the head of John Wesley in her painting of him preaching under a chestnut tree at Rossana. This fine composition captures not only the keen intelligence of Wesley's face and the vast leafy beauty of Rossana's trees, but also the attentive faces of the community which centred on the Tighe family, a community that Maria Spilsbury Taylor came to love. Much later, in July 1815, Maria's husband John Taylor wrote a letter in which he gives his detailed comments:

> The scene is from nature, the name of the place Willybank [Willowbank] so called after a Mr William Tighe who planted the trees which so richly adorn it, and made extensive avenues, also in its neighbourhood. Mr Wesley (whose portrait is copied from Romney's portrait then at Mrs Tighe's where Mrs Taylor was staying) and his Preachers have held quarterly meetings and regularly preached there for many years, and many of the figures in the picture are from life-portraits of worthies who now attend the preaching which I would observe by the way is generally excellent.[7]

John Taylor goes on to identify many of the faces in the painting, amongst them his own three children, Mrs Tighe's brewer and the post-boy, 'a smart, clever youth'.

However, for Mary Blachford and Harry Tighe, who awaited the return of William from his tour abroad, the family's unceasing dedication to Methodism at this time in their lives often seemed tedious and dull. Theodosia was always engaged on a new charitable enterprise. Mary's rejection of the two clergymen selected for her by Theodosia had established that she was not likely to be coerced into a relationship more desirable to her mother than to herself. Theodosia knew she must bide her time. Methodist historian C.H. Crookshank describes Mary's attitude to religion: 'She had a great mental conflict to pass through; for her philosophy and her reading, though they did not pervert her mind, had induced a speculative tendency of reasoning, which inclined towards scepticism.'[8]

Mary was becoming intellectually independent – as her mother wished, a development that brought for Theodosia difficulties she had not anticipated. For Mary, her mother's unbending goodness was hard to challenge. Crookshank writes with glowing praise of all that Theodosia did:

> One of the leading Methodists in Dublin at this period was Mrs Theodosia Blachford, who, having made provision for her children, expended the remainder of a large income chiefly in charity; satisfying herself with few of even the comforts of life, in order to administer to the necessities of others. She spent several hours each day in attending to the education of a number of poor girls, who were not only instructed but also guided and assisted by her in their subsequent progress through life. She was the foundress of an excellent institution called 'The House of Refuge' for unprotected female servants. She also wrote several little tracts, and translated from the French a memoir of the Baroness de Chantal.[9]

The prolific hospitality of the viceregal court, which Mary had so recently sampled under the wing of Aunt Sarah Tighe, provided a painful contrast to the self-inflicted rigours of her mother's mode of existence, yet she had to move from one to the other without comment. She knew from her own observation of life in County Wicklow and in Dublin that her mother was in her own way trying to right the balance amidst all the social wrongs she perceived. The acute inequalities of the age were the crux of the problem. It is significant that in the Methodist Chapel on City Road today there is a memorial to M. de la Flechière's uncle, John Fletcher, who is cited as the man to whom John Wesley had hoped to hand the leadership of the Methodists upon his death. What a perfect union Theodosia had planned between her own daughter and the faith she herself espoused. They soon heard that Fletcher had married another young woman, and Theodosia at last understood that her daughter's decisions were to be her own.

'We removed, at the beginning of 1789 to a pleasant habitation in Gardiner's [*sic*] Row,' wrote Theodosia. She observed her daughter's fading interest in religion and saw that she was troubled by a weakness that had developed at the end of 1788 when 'she was visited with a most extraordinary cough or spasm, every day from two in the afternoon till nine in the evening'. The cough was termed 'nerves'. Advice was taken, for everyone was afraid that this might be tuberculosis: there was an epidemic at this period. The disease was well known but little understood and termed 'phthisis'. 'Our Physician's kindness and attention soothed us daily,' was Theodosia's comment, which unwittingly reveals what was expected of a physician – comforting words that glossed over the real probabilities suggested by the symptoms of disease. 'Partly to break her increasing attachment and to try a change of air, and to obtain the best advice, I took her to London in August 1789, and afterwards by the advice of a Physician there, first to Tonbridge and then to Bath.'[10]

It was in Bath that Mary's condition took a turn for the better just over a year after the illness had begun, and about a year later, the cough had finally gone. The disappearance of this unpleasant symptom convinced the Blachfords that travel to a spa and plenty of rest was the answer to banishing the chestiness they so much feared – and the pattern would be repeated many times in the years to come.

It was during these two years of illness that an invitation came one day from the household at Rossana requesting a visit from the Blachfords. Theodosia writes in her journal:

> In speaking of this period I have omitted a circumstance that had very important consequences. At the latter end of December 1788, when we lodged a little way out of town on account of her cough, Mrs Tighe pressed us to go to Woodstock. I who had always had a secret dread of intimacy with the family, refused positively, but she, who is ever too much keen on carrying her point, sent her carriage and horses all the way to town for us, using at the same time such arguments as induced me against my better impulses to yield rather than seem so positive and ungrateful as to send back the carriage empty. Here we found H. Tighe after a separation of more than two years grown a *very handsome* and captivating young man in his appearance, though only eighteen years of age & here I observed marks of attachment between him and my poor Mary that I determined to break off entirely the proposed, and by me intended, match between her and Mr de la Flechière – To this she willingly consented, but not without some kind of tender regret and denied, I believe without insincerity, that she had any more serious regard for Harry than was warranted by their relationship and intimacy since childhood.[11]

And Mary's loss of faith is noted at this time of the stay at Rossana. Theodosia writes that Harry 'was not religious'. However, she thought him to be a moral young man, and blessed 'with generosity and good nature – an opinion he has never given me good reason to alter'. Theodosia questioned herself over her failure to act more decisively in separating the two young friends, 'Nor did I feel at liberty to put a positive negative on what I then believed to be and in fact really then was her wish.'

Perhaps anyway Theodosia's 'positive negative' would not have been enough to prise apart this developing relationship. Theodosia went with Mary to Rossana again in the summer of 1789 and each time Sarah Tighe came up to Dublin with her son, the two young people met. Mother and daughter remained close, nonetheless:

> She was in a good degree ductile and very affectionate and confiding in her manner to me, and though her religious impressions evidently had declined yet she was sensible to her obligations to me as a mother and a friend and would not in any great instance have departed from their dictates.[12]

Mary's religious journal ends at this point and Theodosia notes her 'literary studies' and her love of poetry and flattery, amply supplied by Henry and his mother.

The early poetry reflects the very same concerns as her journal. In the following poem of August 1789 (she is seventeen) the ideal of spiritual calm is held up as deeply desirable:

> *Happy he whose thoughtful mind*
> *Seeks contentment not on earth,*
> *Not desires nor seeks to find,*
> *Riches, honours, joys or mirth.*
>
> *Far retired from care he lives.*
> *See him calmly, humbly wait,*
> *Peace, beyond what earth e'er gives,*
> *Is the portion of his state.*[13]

Her relationship with her mother is still at times very tender and true. She calls Theodosia 'friend of my heart' as she dedicates a poem to her on her first time away from home:

> *Retired to solitude and soft repose,*
> *To thee I would devote this silent hour;*
> *E'er yet in downy sleep these eyes I close,*
> *Ten thousand blessings on thine head I'd shower.*
>
> *Be thine, dear guardian of my helpless youth,*
> *Friend of my heart, director of my feet,*
> *Be thine each treasure from the fount of truth;*
> *On thee kind heaven distil its comforts sweet.*[14]

But this sweetness of tone was not to last and very soon, in the same year that she praised Theodosia, she wrote a confessional poem, 'From Metastasio', which gives clear voice to her sense of the hollowness of the life she was leading, of the deception she was practising as she feigned happiness – this is the keynote of the poetry and becomes dominant from this point on:

> *Alas! Not only when I write, and sing,*
> *I soar on fancy's ever varying wing.*
> *But all my hopes and all my fears are vain,*
> *And all my acts but like the tales I feign,*
> *Vexed by vain cares, by vain delights deceived,*
> *In empty dreams I joy, and I am grieved:*
> *My raving life is one continual cheat,*
> *And all my wishes but a fond deceit,*
> *Ah Lord! Arouse me from this dream of woes,*
> *And let me in the arms of truth repose.*[15]

Her brother John was less worldly than Mary at this stage. Theodosia writes of his 'first entrance into fashionable vanity' when he, accompanied by 'H Tighe', as Theodosia somewhat curtly terms him, went together to a 'masquerade' or fancy-dress party. Mary helped to dress the two young men who were to ride with three friends to Harristown, twenty miles outside Dublin, for the event. As they left, she quoted (prophetically, her mother thought) from the poet Thomas Gray:

> *Fair laughs the morn, and soft the Zephyr blows,*
> *While proudly riding o'er the azure realm*
> *In gallant trim the gilded vessel goes;*
> *Youth on the prow, and Pleasure at the helm;*

*Regardless of the sweeping whirlwind's sway,*
*That, hushed in grim repose, expects his evening prey…*[16]

A few hours later the young men returned minus one of their number, their clothes soaked in his blood. Highwaymen on the road had attacked them. The injured man was left in town in the care of Solomon Richards, a surgeon and friend of the family. Theodosia lamented this incident which took place just as John came of age: 'poor John's entrance into life has been in respect to punishment, similar to the fate that has ever since attended on him'[17].

But worse was to come, Theodosia records. In May 1792, as had now become their habit, mother and daughter went to stay at Rossana for a summer visit. It was not possible any more to ignore the relationship of Mary and Harry and it seemed to both John and Theodosia that Mary might be 'trifling' or making light of the seriousness with which Harry clearly regarded his cousin's affection. Theodosia spoke out plainly to her daughter. Harry's sister writes in her *Reminiscences* that he became 'so violently attached to her that he threatened to go off to America, or to commit some act of violence, if she refused to marry him'.

At this point the mothers exchanged letters of recrimination. Sarah thought that Mary had exploited Harry's capacity for affection and allowed him to become dependent on her when she did not love him. Theodosia countered her in a letter: 'I consider it a most imprudent step on her side, but still more so on his, as her expectations and desires are far more bounded than his, and what she would think a sufficiency, he would be miserable to submit to.'[18]

It was decided there should be a brief break for reflection. Harry Tighe and John Blachford went off together during the summer of 1792 and travelled in France and Switzerland, as Theodosia said, 'notwithstanding the convulsions which then agitated Europe'. It was hardly a safe time for travel as war had been declared on the Hapsburg dual monarchy of Austria-Hungary in April and passports were required by law for travel in France. In the aftermath of the French Revolution in July 1791, Louis XVI had fled Paris for Varennes and had been brought back a prisoner.

*Henry Tighe and Mary Blachford by Henry Brooke*

The mob in Paris was inflamed by the words of Danton. Unlike his brother William, who continued his journey in other parts of Europe, in November 1792, just before the trial of Louis, Harry decided to go home and with him came his travelling companion, John Blachford. The Terror was soon to begin. They were frightened by what they had seen. Might the unrest at home follow the French pattern? They talked throughout their rough sea passage of whether such an uprising could take place in Ireland. They wondered as well if William would be safe in his travels. Harry began to realise why his mother had been anxious on his departure. He thought of his home at Rossana and of his cousin Mary. He had seen a society in chaos and he felt the tremors of upheaval begin to affect his own life.

The travellers went to Rossana immediately upon their return. Harry had decided to claim Mary's hand. Cousin Caroline said categorically: 'Mary did not love him . . .' And where Theodosia said that she believed him to be 'moral', Caroline doubted that this was the case, her sharp tone cutting through the arguments to the truth of the matter. All that was left for Theodosia was 'anxiety, sorrow and terror' through the winter of 1792 and the summer of 1793:

> …while I saw my poor child struggling with a foolish and violent passion half insensible to the tenderness of a heart that she was unwilling, indeed seemingly unable to wound by a positive refusal, though she saw her favourite lover at her feet in rank and fortune unexceptionable & her equal, at the same time confessing to me her reluctance to any closer connection with H Tighe.[19]

The 'favourite lover' is identified by Caroline Hamilton as 'T. Singleton, afterwards married to Lord T's daughter and settled in England'. Research suggests that perhaps he came from the Singletons of Ardee, Co. Louth, or from the branch of the family at Aclare, Co. Meath. A mysterious diary entry of 1 December 1795 runs:

> My life was embittered to me – some tidings I heard that made me loath the light and long to be concealed in the peaceful silent tomb, which holds all that our ancestors loved so much of what was once so dear to ourselves.[20]

What tidings were these? Had Mary heard of the engagement of a Captain Singleton to Mary Bourke? They would marry early the next year as is recorded in Walker's *Hibernian Magazine* in the index to marriages. Or was her 'favourite lover' James Singleton, son of Sydenham Singleton who married Caroline Upton in 1804? There is no further information in her diary about Singleton, but Mary's poetry is full of a 'secret grief' in which perhaps this brief courtship plays a part.

Harry had other ideas. He had fallen in love with Mary Blachford, much to the disapproval of her mother. Mary would find herself without the power to resist this person, part-cousin, part-lover, already close of kin, who seemed as familiar as the milk she always drank for breakfast, as comforting as a playmate who could always be relied upon to entertain her and as fashionably sensitive as his brother was full of common sense.

Despite the loss of their husbands, Sarah Tighe and Theodosia Blachford had tried hard to fulfil their ambitions for their children and now they were full of misgivings about the relationship. Their correspondence is angry, each accusing the other of giving the young bad advice. Sarah had more generosity of spirit perhaps, and found room for tolerance, but Theodosia never forgave her and found it hard to have patience with the two young people who were falling so precipitately into a lifelong relationship.

NOTES

1 Sonnet: 'As the frail bark, long tossed by stormy winds', March 1791.
2 *Journal of Mary Tighe*: NLI 4810.
3 One of Wesley's favourite sayings: Zechariah 3:2.
4 John Wesley: *A Short Method of Converting all the Roman Catholics in the Kingdom of Ireland. Humbly proposed to the Bishops and Clergy of this Kingdom*: published Dublin, 1752.
5 *Journal of John Wesley*, 1762.
6 *Journal of John Wesley*, 1789.
7 Letter from John Taylor, July 1815.
8 C.H.Crookshank: *History of Methodism in Ireland*, 1886.
9 ibid.
10 Theodosia Blachford: *Observations on the Journal of Mary Tighe*, NLI 4810.
11 ibid.
12 ibid.
13 Poem: 'True happiness is only found', 1789.
14 Poem: 'To her Mother at Rossana', 1791.
15 Poem: 'From Metastasio', 1791.
16 'The Bard' by Thomas Gray, 1757.
17 Theodosia Blachford: *Observations on the Journal of Mary Tighe*, NLI 4810.
18 Letter from Theodosia Blachford to Sarah Tighe, 1792.
19 Theodosia Blachford: *Observations on the Journal of Mary Tighe*, NLI 4810.
20 *Journal of Mary Tighe*: NLI 4810.

# CHAPTER 5

# IN LONDON
## *'Also a poetess'*

Mary Blachford Tighe's life contained inherent contradictions of which she was conscious but which she was unable to resolve. Perhaps at this point the poet who had voyaged in the frail bark of Mary's soul emerged and grew a little stronger and more confident of being able to tell her story. In her journal the night before she married, she made the following entry:

4 October 1793

My soul draws back with terror and awe at the idea of the event that is to take place tomorrow. Oh My God! Let it not be unattended with thy blessing.[1]

*Henry Tighe, after George Romney*

It was as if the magnitude of this life-changing event had crept upon her unawares, and inward happiness was hard to achieve. Mary felt insecure and to live in Ireland permanently did not seem acceptable. She longed to travel but Harry had neither income of his own nor any means of earning. The problems of being the second son weighed on his shoulders and, despite a correspondence with his older brother about settling in the neighbourhood, Harry decided to fend for himself and for his wife and to go away, for a while at least. The newly wed couple set out for England where Harry was to continue his studies for the Bar.

London was prosperous in the last quarter of the eighteenth century and the Thames bristled with the masts of ships trading overseas. In the city new houses were built and there was a movement westwards for the better off as well as northwards away from the narrow streets of the centre where most business still took place, while the poor moved eastwards. It was an age of flourishing public life, when it was fashionable to go out to the coffee houses, assemblies, clubs of all kinds, balls, pleasure gardens, concerts and above all else to the theatre. Social life was conducted in public and this suited the young Tighes for the moment.

At first Henry enjoyed such entertainment to the full: assemblies and literary soirées, visits to the Pleasure Gardens at Vauxhall and to the theatre captured his imagination and he found that circulating with his pretty and clever young wife was infinitely preferable to time spent in chambers and at his books. He did qualify as a barrister in 1796 but he does not appear to have practised and he admitted that he did not feel he had chosen the right career. To keep her dream of writing alive, Mary continued to think of herself as a poet and to write when she could. Harry's school friends from Harrow provided hospitality in London to discuss literary subjects and admire his pretty wife, 'now idle young lawyers' according to his sister Caroline, whose comments on her brother at this stage are disparaging:

> Her husband soon abandoned the prospect of rising at the Bar and as he saw no probability of having a family, he sought only for amusement for himself and his wife at water drinking places, in England during some summers and in Dublin during several winters. He spent an idle life, at home, reading for amusement, not profit, and associating with those only with whom he felt perfectly at his ease. I often thought him much to be pitied as he saw that his wife did not love him, though he loved her.[2]

Caroline coldly makes this last statement about her brother, Henry: he loved Mary – but he knew that this love was not reciprocated. This is certainly the truth of the matter. Her tender nature had drawn back 'with terror and awe' the night before she was married for in her heart of hearts she knew her love for Harry was not sufficient to respond to his. And Theodosia was always to hand because she too knew that this was the truth of the matter:

> Her anxious mother always lived in a small lodging near her, continually praying for her and always ready to go to her in an evening if she happened to have no engagement to take her from home. At such times she used to work while her mother or husband read to her if one or two of her nearest relations were not there to join in easy pleasant conversation which in her family (more than any other I have since been acquainted with) never flagged.[3]

Mary's scholarly habits learned in childhood did not desert her: 'she always rose early to read for some hours before her companions in dissipation were awake, which her poor mother thought was one means of undermining her health, as she never seemed refreshed by sleep.' This is a very telling comment, revealing as it does the underlying grief of the newly married Mary. She was dissatisfied, uneasy in her conscience, unable to concentrate on what she really wanted to do. And the world of London entertainment beckoned enticingly every evening, offering her much longed for experience of the world. Her mother's fear that burning the candle at both ends in this way was bad for her daughter's health was no doubt well founded and it is not difficult to imagine Theodosia's dilemma: should she advise the young people yet again to pace themselves more carefully, or was it best to refrain from giving advice because that in itself might provoke rebellion. One of Mary's time and energy-consuming activities was learning Latin. She had not been taught this subject as a child, but Harry had been well schooled at Harrow. She persuaded him against his inclination to help her each day and soon made good progress. The exercise gave them both pleasure and allowed him to take the intellectual initiative.

Perhaps from the time her daughter was quite small, Theodosia had underestimated her capacity for rebellion, not realising that she operated on low-level resistance. She allowed her mother to perceive her as 'ductile', while making her own effort to move out into the world to gain experience in her own right. Mary Wollstonecraft's *Vindication of the Rights of Woman*, which was published in 1792, attacked the 'mistaken notions of female excellence', which allowed women of the day to cultivate a passive image that would fit in with the male notion of femininity. Theodosia sensed that Mary perhaps even blamed the older generation. Cousin Caroline wrote: 'Her poor mother bitterly repented to the last hour of her life, having given her consent to this marriage.'[4]

Theodosia's own marriage was short but sweet and this provided a painful contrast to the relationship she saw unfolding before her as from one month to the next she followed the young couple around London and the spas. The following account written in London in 1792 gives Theodosia's recollection of her own early happiness and grief at her husband's unexpectedly early death:

> Great God! What a scene of intoxication does the three years of my wedded life now appear! How perfect was my felicity! And yet how insensible was I of it! How did his tenderness, indulgence and unbounded confidence more than answer my fondest expectations! He was indeed the friend and lover! Daily encreasing [sic] affection, uninterrupted cheerfulness and grateful acknowledgement of perfect happiness was what I never failed to meet with from him. But how is this felicity now vanished like the baseless fabric of a vision! And I am left to struggle with homelessness, sorrows and difficulties.
>
> Alas, I have no friend now to complain to. All connections appear so insipid when compared to that which providence has broken. I seem to myself a single unconnected being . . . But what I suffer in waking hours is trifling to that which I endure in sleep. He is then always present with me, yet is there generally a something which makes me sensible that what I enjoy is but a phantom.[5]

Had Mary married a man who could have provided her with a stable home and a place to live, it would have been very much to the benefit of her mother as well as herself. But this was not to be and Theodosia hovered uncertainly around the young couple. They did not take her out on all their expeditions. The many distractions of the city of London provided Mr and Mrs Henry Tighe with diversions enough for the following two or three years. The delights of the Pleasure Gardens were open to them.

*The Pleasure Gardens at Vauxhall by Thomas Rowlandson*

The Spring Gardens of Vauxhall which had been a day out for Samuel Pepys and his family was quite as entertaining for the Tighes. Mr and Mrs Pepys went by water in the seventeenth century and most visitors took a boat in the eighteenth century. One would be hired and the party landed at Vauxhall jetty, jostling dangerously with disembarking passengers. Once in the Pleasure Gardens, food and drink was purchased and walks taken amongst the many trees and gardens which gave the pleasant illusion of rural bliss without all the trouble of driving out of town to the countryside. It took just a short time to get there, and all society was present to be observed. The fact that it was not permitted for a gentleman to take his retinue of servants with him into the Gardens conferred a temporary equality upon everyone present and behind the anonymity of a masque anyone might take liberties. There was a Vauxhall Gardens in Paris, and indeed at Versailles Marie Antoinette's pastoral games of dressing as a milkmaid on her so-called farm were undertaken in a spirit close to the masquerades at the London gardens. This was a classless environment where social barriers dissolved, just for an evening. Here were thousands of little oil lights which were illuminated to thrilling effect as darkness fell. In Dublin there were several public places where people gathered on fine evenings – St Stephen's

Green and the Rotunda Gardens, but nothing as impressive as this show. Evelina, the eponymous hero of Fanny Burney's novel, goes alone into the 'dark alleys' of Vauxhall and is saved from unwelcome advances by an admirer. To justify the outing to Theodosia, the young Tighes said they were going to a concert to hear some music. Handel wrote a special hornpipe for Vauxhall and the orchestra often played 'The Dead March' from *Saul*. Now that Westminster Bridge had been reopened, it was no longer necessary to go to Vauxhall Gardens by water, a carriage could be taken across the bridge and down the South Bank to the entrance.

It seems likely that Harry sometimes went alone, for there are indications that he grew impatient with his serious, yet vacillating wife. And she, too, went her own way. At about this time – 1794 – Mary Tighe was painted by the fashionable portraitist George Romney who was in his day considered the equal of Thomas Gainsborough, Sir Joshua Reynolds and Thomas Lawrence. Romney had painted Harry's brother just before he left Eton – why should she not sit for him too? It is an indication of Mary's developing sense of self-worth that she made this decision as a young society woman and as a writer. An account of family history narrates that Romney much admired her and that she sat without her husband's knowledge.

When presented with the bill, which was for £30, Harry refused to pay since he had not been consulted in the matter. Henry Grattan, the family friend and parliamentarian, offered to purchase the portrait, which now hangs in the National Gallery of Ireland.

Mary did go to the theatre, as Caroline Hamilton dramatically relates:

Though her mother had permitted her to go to some assemblies, she had never been to the Theatre and I remember the first time he proposed to take her there. I was with her. He had taken us one evening, out in a carriage and we knew not where we were going, when we stopped at Drury Lane. She remonstrated, wept, fearing to grieve her poor mother, who had followed her to London and lived in the house with her and, who, justly, had a great prejudice against all Theatrical amusements. But Mary had no firmness to resist persuasion and she was so much delighted with Bannister and Mrs. Siddons that from that time she went frequently to the Play house.[6]

*Mary Tighe by George Romney*

As regards the stage, Theodosia Blachford's moral position was that of a Methodist: she deeply disapproved. The London theatres at this time were popular and full of talented actors and playwrights. The Drury Lane Theatre, to which Caroline says Henry took them, was the most famous. David Garrick, actor and manager, had been bought out at the Drury Lane by the playwright, Richard Brinsley Sheridan, who put on his early plays here. When the young Tighes purchased their tickets to see John Bannister and Mrs Siddons and later 'went frequently to the Playhouse', they had plenty of fine performances from which to choose. There was the Little Theatre in the Haymarket, a big and new theatre at Sadler's Wells which replaced the old music house, Astley's. In addition, in 1794 The Lyceum at the east end of the Strand became a playhouse, while The Royal Circus was fitted out for plays. The Royalty Theatre had opened its doors in 1787 near the Tower of London and Covent Garden had been restructured and enlarged in 1792. Such a hub of drama could be reached by carriage in the evening from Manchester Square, just north of Oxford Street, when they stayed in Sarah Tighe's house. As well as plays by Shakespeare and the well-known English dramatists, new ones increasingly dealt with contemporary events and political issues. For instance, in the same year as the French Revolution, a play was put on entitled *The Destruction of the Bastille and the Triumph of Liberty*. And in 1793 *The Royal Prisoners of France* was on at Covent Garden. Tickets were hard to come by because what had happened in France was of great public interest.

Kemble's intense performances of Shakespeare's tragic heroes were drawing full houses and to Mary, who had read the plays, this was pure pleasure as well as stimulus for the poetic imagination. Kemble worked up his studies of character through a single line in the text and developed from there a thought-provoking interpretation such as London theatregoers had never seen before. His sister Mrs Siddons played Lady Macbeth to his Macbeth in her special complementary style. She had learned her craft with the York and Bath Companies before making her sensational return to Drury Lane in 1782. Sometimes the elder members of the Kemble family played together – John Philip, Stephen, Charles and Sarah Siddons, a most expressive actor, who told Thomas Moore, the Irish poet and actor, that she stored the emotions required for her part in her memory and that she had always found in acting a vent for her private feelings. The young theatre-goers got together after the play to discuss the production. Such concern with the working of the mind appealed to Mary Tighe especially, and she stored ideas for the writing of 'Psyche; or, The Legend of Love'.

*Mrs Siddons and Philip Kemble*
*in* Macbeth

As the experience of Henry and Mary Tighe widened in scope, they became accustomed to being known as a married couple and their mutual understanding grew. But in fact they became more like brother and sister – they were after all first cousins. Mary felt herself to be different from most other young women she met; she could not share discussions about children and the best way to deal with the problem was to avoid the subject. Cousin Caroline says firmly that Henry 'saw no probability of having a family'. The certainty of this utterance suggests that Mary may have suffered from amenorrhoea. Perhaps she was already aware that her consumptive state would not allow her to have a child – she was underweight and simply not strong enough.

It was on one of their journeys from Ireland that the young couple paused for a few days in north Wales to visit the celebrated Ladies of Llangollen. The Tighes were distantly related to Sarah Ponsonby. The Tighe children had grown up hearing the somewhat scandalous yet exciting tale of the escape of the two women from Ireland to Llangollen and they were acutely aware of its significance in family mythology. The Ladies lived in a little rural paradise free from the pressures created by mothers, husbands or lovers. Sarah Ponsonby and Eleanor Butler had first attempted to flee from their families in County Kilkenny in 1778. Both were young women from Ascendancy families who resisted attempts by their parents to make them marry 'suitable' young men whose titles would perpetuate the inheritance of the Ponsonbys, the Fownes and the Butlers of Kilkenny Castle. They eloped together with due drama and were successful only on the second attempt to escape from their irate relations and thus opt out of the Irish marriage market. After much deliberation, they settled at Llangollen in north Wales. However, in leaving their families, the Ladies cut themselves off from their inheritance and were resigned to living modestly. They were at first dependent upon the charity of Sarah Tighe of Rossana in the same way as Mary and Harry: they relied on her making suitable financial arrangements for their income. In her own haphazard way, Sarah Tighe was very generous and she sent the Ladies money and provided a stipend of £80 per annum, even when she herself was short of funds.

*Plas Newydd, Llangollen today*

The reason for this was that her parents, Sir William and Lady Fownes of Woodstock, had as a deed of kindness adopted the orphaned child of a cousin, Sarah Ponsonby, and invited her to live permanently with them.

After a lonely and unhappy childhood, Sarah Ponsonby (or Sally, as she was known in the family) settled at first at Woodstock, the house on the hill at Inistioge. While at boarding school, she had already met Lady Eleanor Butler, youngest of the three daughters of Walter Butler, head of the Ormonde family, who became Earl of Ormonde in 1766. Lady Eleanor's home was Kilkenny Castle which was only sixteen miles away from Woodstock. The two young women became close friends. And there was another dimension to the story. The elderly Sir William Fownes, who had apparently so generously adopted the orphan Sally, now took another kind of interest in her: gouty and bad-tempered, he still had ambitions of a male heir and was planning that when his wife died he would take a younger woman and fulfil his wish – Miss Ponsonby might be useful here. He let his attentions be known and the young woman found herself in a painfully embarrassing position. Loyal to Lady Betty Fownes, who had

*The Ladies of Llangollen*

adopted her in a time of need and who had been as a mother to her, Sarah Ponsonby did not know where to turn:

> . . . neither my pride, resentment, nor any other passion shall ever be sufficiently powerful to make me give Lady Betty any uneasiness in my power to spare her, and I sometimes laugh to think of the earnestness with which she presses me to be obliging to him, for I have adopted the most reserved mode of behaviour ever since.[7]

Eleanor from Kilkenny Castle was someone to tell, a sympathetic ear. Bright, independent, disenchanted with family life, Lady Eleanor Butler listened to her younger, inexperienced friend and thus they came to think up a plan for escape. It was poor Lady Betty who was upset by the loss of her adopted child. She wrote to Mrs Goddard: 'My dear Goddard, I cant

*Lady Elizabeth Fownes and Sir William Fownes*

paint our distress. Our dear Sally lept out of a window last night and is gone off.'

Less than two months after the dramatic elopement of Sarah Ponsonby and Eleanor Butler, Sir William died in great pain as the result of disease of the stomach caused by an unidentified illness, which some termed guilt. So he predeceased his wife, whom he had prematurely planned to replace, but only by a few weeks. Lady Betty Fownes followed him swiftly to the grave and thus both Sarah Tighe's parents died and she inherited the family seat, Woodstock.

Travellers passing *en route* turned off the road to visit the Ladies of Llangollen in their extended and beautifully furnished house now complete with library, dairy and well-tended gardens. They corresponded with politicians and literary men and women of the day and went out to visit the local gentry, though they nearly always returned at night to their 'silent and still cottage' travelling by the light of the moon or of Jupiter. Wordsworth and Southey, members of the Darwin family, Sir Walter Scott, the Duke of Wellington and Sir Humphrey Davey were among some of their many visitors. In August 1795, Henry and Mary

Tighe were invited and their visit is recorded with a note on Mary's charms and a comment that she was 'also a poetess'.

Harry got on well with the Ladies and joked about the fact they had in common with him a meagre inheritance and had to remind his mother when their allowance was due, just as he did, though in fact neither party was poor by the standards of the day: they all planned to go to Botany Bay together if funds ran out entirely. Mary was admired as a beautiful young woman and the very fact that they were invited on the same day as Anna Seward, poet and writer, was in itself a compliment. The small paradise created by the two industrious ladies seemed enviable to Mary Tighe as she contemplated the way in which she herself had been brought up to believe that she must take a male partner. How brave these women had been to defy convention, how courageous to give up entirely the country of their birth and start from nothing on their own. They enjoyed an even-handed, trusting relationship in which everything was discussed, from the purchase of a cow to the literary value of a poem by a writer. Such domestic felicity seemed to Mary to be in marked contrast to her own unhappy peregrinations around fashionable watering places. The Ladies hobnobbed with the locals, much as they might have done in Ireland, and were always hospitable. This place of rural safety seemed very desirable to Mary and she kept the memory of it in her heart until 1809 when the ravages of consumption gave her little option to travel any more and she left Dublin to live in the beauty of the countryside at Woodstock.

Should Mary perhaps have remained single? There were a growing number of literary women who turned askance from the demands of married life. One such was Anna Seward, who lived in Lichfield and would die just a year before Mary Tighe. As a young woman Anna Seward fell in love with a married man, the conductor of the Lichfield cathedral choir and after this affair ended she made a conscious decision not to search for another. She was in her late forties when the Ladies of Llangollen invited the young Tighes to meet her. Anna Seward was a poet and novelist and perhaps a model for Mary in this dual role. Sir Walter Scott edited her poetical works in three volumes and he wrote an introduction, together with a selection of extracts

*Anna Seward by Tilly Kettle*

from her correspondence. She wrote the life of Erasmus Darwin who lived in the town of Lichfield, which was also the birthplace of Dr Johnson, who knew her well. As a climax to Miss Seward's visit in August 1795, the Ladies arranged for her to accompany them on a grand picnic given by their friend Mrs Ormsby in the beautiful ruins of the Valle Crucis Abbey, only two miles away in green fields below the steep mountains of Llangollen. Fastidious preparations were made and a large meal was prepared to be eaten on the

*Valle Crucis Abbey*

grass. The poet called the scenery 'silent, impressive, awful'. A harpist had been hired and the picnickers' appreciation of the 'sublime' grew as the afternoon waned and the Welsh mountains reflected the evening light. They all returned exhilarated to Llangollen in the three chaises and two phaetons hired especially for the occasion.

This encounter with 'the poetess' was very important for Mary Tighe whose intellectual circles had been narrow up until then. She had heard tell of the bluestocking circle of men and women who met to talk about contemporary issues and to promote their own intellectual well-being, she had heard of the literary hosts in London at whose houses the group gathered for their discussions, but she had not met with many English writers. The bluestocking meetings included men such as Samuel Johnson, Edmund Burke and David Garrick. The term 'bluestocking' was coined when the scholar Benjamin Stillingfleet arrived at Elizabeth Montagu's house dressed in the blue worsted stockings usually worn by working men rather than the white silk stockings then fashionable. James Boswell, in his life of Dr Johnson, tells us that when Stillingfleet was away, someone remarked that nothing could be done without the 'bluestockings'. Later on, Mary Tighe was termed a 'bluestocking' by Thomas Moore, though he did not intend the term to be entirely complimentary.

Between visits to England, they returned to Ireland and to Rossana. William Howitt in his *Homes and Haunts of the British Poets* (1847) cites an account given by a curate visiting Rossana who was clearly impressed by the outward flourishes with which the family lived and by the pure handsomeness of the young, newly married couple. He visited when the chestnut trees were in full leaf and the lawns and flowerbeds of Rossana at their best. The Revd S. Pierce wrote to his wife in July 1796 about his hostess, Sarah Tighe:

> She has three sons; one has a seat in the House of Parliament; the youngest lives with her; another, Mr. Henry Tighe, having lately married, is building himself a house near his mother's. Of all the men I ever saw, I never was so much interested at the glance of a moment as when my eyes first fell on him. I fancied I perceived all the dignity and frankness of a Roman in his face and bearing; nor was I disappointed. I found him the idol of his acquaintance...his lady is young, lovely and of sweet manners, united with as sweet a form. She entered the room soon after I came to Rossana with a chaplet of roses about her head. 'Where', I thought, 'were the beauties of the garden and the parlour so united before?' Indeed, I felt myself as on enchanted ground, amused with a pleasing dream, too romantic to be true.[8]

*Rossana Cottage, photograph 1883, Irish Architectural Archive*

From the context in which the Revd Pierce writes of 'a house near his mother's', it would appear that Henry was building on the estate and near to Rossana. The cottage, now called The Dower House, then called Rossana Cottage, is within walking distance and of suitable size for the second son of the house. Perhaps Sarah thought that she herself might live there one day when Mary and Henry had children and wished to move into Rossana. As a home for Mary and Henry, the cottage seems perfect. Of elegant proportions and with the River Vartry meandering around the edge of the garden, it is not difficult to imagine the young couple making plans to settle there sooner rather than later.

Life had certainly become more interesting. Mary was well entertained. The Revd Pierce gives us a captivating portrait of the young couple on the lawns at Rossana, he so handsome, she wearing roses winningly in her hair, both absorbed in planning their new house. But her soul retreated a little the night before she married, and it had not, as yet, come entirely out of hiding.

NOTES

1 *Journal of Mary Tighe*: NLI 4810.
2 Caroline Hamilton: *Mary Tighe*, NLI 4810.
3 ibid.
4 ibid.
5 *Written by Mrs Blachford after her husband's death, 14 July 1773*: NLI 4810.
6 Caroline Hamilton: *Mary Tighe*, NLI 4810.
7 Letter from Sarah Ponsonby to Lucy Goddard: Wicklow Papers 4239.
8 Revd Pierce, letter to his wife, 1796 quoted by William Howitt, *Homes and Haunts of the British Poets,* Routledge, 1847.

# CHAPTER 6

# THE SEARCH FOR HEALTH
## *'Like the worn sand'*

The deteriorating health of Mary Blachford Tighe is reflected in the movement of the young couple from one English spa to another in search of good air and the benefits of waters in whose purity and mineral qualities many hopes were placed. Mary was fragile, as Harry Tighe knew, but he had never before held responsibility for her health as he did now and he found himself suddenly involved with her in a new way. When they went to Bath, Theodosia was not with them and Mary fell ill with 'what is called the influenza'. She writes to her 'dearest Mama and Sally' (Sarah Tighe) from Park Street, Bath, on 14 March 1794:

> We are still here, notwithstanding the time fix'd on for our removal from the town is long since past – and yet I hardly know why we have staid so long for this place is certainly tiresome with very few attractions for Harry – The kindness we have experienced however from our relations has made it very agreeable to us and I shall always love Bath for making me so well known to Lady Anne, Arabella and their very amiable families. I have never heard of a more sickly season than the present – There is not, I believe a family in Bath that has escaped the general illness. I am but just recovered from a most severe visit of what is called the influenza. During four days in which I was confined to my bed I really think I suffered more pain than in all the rest of my life. I however got rid of it with my fever in one night and was suddenly almost well in moment – and I am however still very weak and am much altered by it in my looks – Poor Harry is the best of Nurse-tenders. I trust I may soon have an opportunity of showing

my gratitude by a return of his kind attention in the same manner... Harry desires me to excuse his not writing but I tell him I don't know how this is to be done. He promises a letter very soon and sends his love.[1]

There was sympathy and affection between the young people. Their relationship was becoming more rewarding as Mary realised how tenderly he felt for her and she recognised her need for him. But the role of nurse did not come easily to Harry Tighe, nor did the role of responsible reporter to the family – his letter-writing skills had never been great. William was the one in the family who could write fluently. Soon Theodosia joined them in their travels, sometimes staying in accommodation nearby, sometimes under the same roof. After Bath came Exmouth, and then they went back to London: 'I have few friends in London whom I expect to meet with much pleasure and yet I cannot help considering it as a place which will certainly afford the charms of an agreeable society.'[2]

When the visits to Drury Lane Theatre and the London Pleasure Gardens palled, it is interesting to see that the Tighes, in common with many of the young offspring of similar eighteenth-century Irish families, did not settle in anywhere in England but perched like birds, resting for a while, and then moving on. They went from one relation to another, always looking for an Irish connection. July 1795 found them staying with Mary's mother's family at Cobham in Surrey, one of the seats of the Earl of Darnley. It was here that they got news of the death of their friend, Thomas James Fortescue of Ravensdale Park. He had died in dramatic and unexplained circumstances after crossing the Irish Sea by boat. Did he suffer ill-effects from the journey? Was he poisoned by some kind of palliative medicine that he took against sea-sickness? This young man seemed typical of their kind and his death disturbed them:

Indeed, I cannot banish from my mind the melancholy end of him, whom I do not now scruple to call my friend, how remarkable is it that the very last morning I saw him he should express much terror and reluctance at going to Ireland and that he should, indeed, only land on Saturday and be no more on Monday. From what I can gather, I fear very much that he owes his death to some medicine taken by mistake – Surely, in the midst of life we are in death![3]

One of seven children, Fortescue had three brothers and three sisters. His father, the Right Hon. James Fortescue, sat in the Irish Parliament first for Dundalk and then in 1761 he was returned for County Louth. His son Thomas followed in his footsteps as MP and it was in this capacity that Mary and Harry knew him from their Dublin days, and from social events at the Castle. The Fortescue boys were of similar stock, had shared the same rural Irish childhoods; they too had felt their Irish responsibilities casting a shadow over their time of youthful leisure in England. They all knew that sooner or later they would have to return. Within three years, Henry Tighe would be riding with the Yeomanry through the Hills of Wicklow in the 1798 Rebellion. Thomas Fortescue's younger brother George, Rector of Killala, would die in County Mayo as the result of his wounds when the French landed there in support of the Irish rebels in August 1798. Mary's diary entry for 25 July 1795 reads:

> Heard of Fortescue's death – Oh my God, I bow in reverence to thy awful and afflicting dispensations – but spare thy worm! Cut me not off in the midst of my sins – spare me a little that I may recover my strength before I go hence and am no more seen. Oh! Thou soul of my departed friend, where art thou? Hast thou found mercy?[4]

The two halves of Mary's personality converge suddenly in conflict: her religious upbringing and the pleasure-loving self. Is she prepared for her creator? Is she ready to die? The teaching of her mother is deeply ingrained in her consciousness and fights battle with the emerging independent young woman of the new age. The often perilous journey from Holyhead became for Mary Tighe the very symbol of her own precarious existence. It would have been possible to return to Rossana. Their cottage was nearly ready and they could live apart from the family. But to Harry this seemed an admission of defeat. He had not made his own way in the world, and he did not wish to be seen merely as his mother's dependant. They moved on yet again to another town, this time Cheltenham, and here Mary wrote a sonnet in which she addresses Death. She was twenty-three.

*O thou most terrible, most dreaded power,*
*In whatsoever form thou meetest the eye!*
*Whether thou biddest the sudden arrow fly*
*In the dread silence of the midnight hour;*
*Or whether, hovering o'er the lingering wretch*
*The sad cold javelin hangs suspended long,*
*While round the couch the weeping kindred throng*
*With hope and fear alternately on stretch;*
*Oh, say, for me what horrors are prepared?*
*Am I now doomed to meet thy fateful arm?*
*Or wilt thou first from life steal every charm,*
*And bear away each good my soul would guard?*
*That thus, deprived of all it loved, my heart*
*From life itself contentedly may part?*[5]

The poet perceives the random nature of accidental death and the palpable fear of dying young can be seen and felt. Mary has dwelt upon the death of Thomas Fortescue and her sensitive nature converts his experience into anticipation of her own end, whenever it will be.

In 1796 the family was to go to Scarborough, for Mary's brother John Blachford was engaged and he and his nineteen-year-old bride-to-be were to come to the seaside town to meet her new family. They were hoping to find a suitable house for him, but as yet the search was unsuccessful: 'Nothing at all has offer'd and this coast is so bleak that Harry is much inclin'd to give over any further search on this side of England and talks of trying the coast of Lancashire for something more sheltered.'

Harry often wanted to move on when the rest of the party was content to stay in the same place. Their way of life lacked security. Harry's wish reflects his natural good health and the restlessness that arose from a lack of employment. He had no purpose in life except to enjoy himself. Mary, on the other hand, was now suffering from lowering bouts of breathing difficulties and was frankly unable to keep up with her energetic young husband. However, she liked Scarborough, or so she said:

Scarboro' itself is, in my opinion, extremely beautiful. We have very comfortable lodgings and as I never before lived directly within full view of the sea I find it a never-failing amusement – Indeed I could not have believed that there was such an infinite variety in an object which at a distance appears with such tiresome sameness – I have from my window a view of the open sea and a beautiful harbour – without the disadvantage of a river which the tide entirely carries away. I hate that circumstance and would rather have no sea at all than have it only for a few hours with a bare strand the remaining part of the day. Mama is in the house with us here which in itself is a gratification which I may not have in our next residence – you know how much she likes going her own way.[6]

The tone is somewhat petulant as regards the behaviour of tidal rivers but it is not hard to detect a solid determination to make the most of what she has – a quality her husband seems to have lacked. And the back-up provided by Theodosia is clearly welcome. But the poem written here in Scarborough reveals a quite different side to her nature: there is a profound awareness of the transience of life, as well as a new confidence in handling the sonnet as an expressive form which places her amongst some of the best poets of the period:

> *As musing pensive in my silent home*
> *I hear far off the sullen ocean's roar,*
> *Where the rude wave just sweeps the level shore,*
> *Or bursts upon the rocks with whitening foam,*
> *I think upon the scenes my life has known;*
> *On days of sorrow and some hours of joy;*
> *Both which alike time could so soon destroy!*
> *And now they seem a busy dream alone;*
> *While on the earth exists no single trace*
> *Of all that shook my agitated soul,*
> *As on the beach new waves for ever roll*
> *And fill their past forgotten brother's place:*
> *But I, like the worn sand, exposed remain*
> *To each new storm which frets the angry main.[7]*

We hear the 'sullen ocean's roar' and feel the poet's sense of impotence in face of such relentless power. Some of her best poetry has the simplicity of this sonnet with its paired monosyllables, 'rude wave', 'new waves', 'worn sand', 'new storm'. Just two sentences move through the poem with the power of the ocean itself. Mary Tighe reveals her own acute sense of vulnerability when she compares herself to the worn, exposed sand awaiting the ravages of the next storm. The petulant if reflective girl of the letter is replaced by a mature young woman who knows already what her situation is and can express her fears with an eloquent simplicity.

Harry had his way and the search for lodgings was abandoned in Scarborough. Harry, Mary and Theodosia made a long and tiring journey across country to Wales and on down to Swansea where the weather was better and lodgings were found for everyone. Arrangements were made to welcome John and Camilla, and Mary was so excited about the first encounter that she found it hard to sleep for several nights as she dreamed of their meeting. Her fondness for her brother is palpable in her letter to Aunt Sarah, as is her already pronounced depression, or 'gloom' as she terms it: 'Harry exclaimed there is John and in an instant I was in his arms...there are not many such moments in life and if it were not for these precious bright spots who could endure the gloom?'[8]

Behind John stood Camilla. She was perhaps Swiss, but spoke good English –'She speaks almost like a native of England'.[9] John met her when travelling abroad and his mother had had no chance to vet his choice, so they were anxious to meet her: 'I am too much of a woman not to begin with her person – tho' she is certainly not handsome yet I can hardly say she has no pretensions to any kind of beauty because I am sure many people would call her a fine woman and her countenance is animated and very agreeable – perfectly good-humoured – she is much taller than I am and very large, but has not at all a masculine appearance.' Mary damns her sister-in-law with faint praise, qualifying every compliment with a negative: 'a very large mouth is not, I think, ugly', and 'she certainly wears no rouge'.[10]

Camilla and John Blachford settled down in Swansea for a honeymoon and everyone enjoyed the happy conviviality. Because they were for once gathered as a family, they were more like other people there, although they were living in temporary accommodation. They paid visits to each other every day and Theodosia's joy at having her children together enhanced every outing. To these days they must all have often returned in their memories, for the happiness of John and Camilla was not to last.

This restless lifestyle was having a painful effect on Mary Tighe's health. She felt increasingly unwell. Out of season, the resorts were sad places and Harry's lack of employment lay heavily upon them both. He claimed he did not wish to work, yet he was singularly restless when at home. His frustrated energy contrasted cruelly with her languor. Her mind returned to William on his estate at Woodstock, to Sarah comfortably busy at Rossana. She herself had no fixed abode, no certain sense of identity, while the family continued to travel from one health resort to another. They had spent time in London and seen what was on offer by way of social life. They had lived for short periods in several of the English spas with the justification that Mary's health must come first and that to take the waters was beneficial, but Harry was evidently restless now and heard news of his home in Wicklow with some trepidation. The 1790s were uneasy times even without a consumptive wife and, as second-in-line to a very capable brother, Harry felt inclined to want to get back to see where he stood at home.

Irish matters did not dominate conversation at the spa in Bath or in Scarborough or on the elegant pavements of Cheltenham but Harry and Mary Tighe heard the news nonetheless in letters from their friends and relations and it seemed to have a power of magnetic force. Mary felt increasingly curious about William, his rootedness, his confidence. He had not wandered like some kind of modern pilgrim through the spas of England. What would be his view of the political situation? The couple had three children, born between 1794 and 1797. He was, she had heard, happily married to Marianne Gahan, the daughter of Daniel Gahan, MP for Fethard, Co. Tipperary. But there was a double bind: in some ways the Tighes looked forward to returning to a country that spoke so comfortably of affluence and security, that seemed to be burgeoning, yet they knew that this message was not to be trusted and that some kind of political uprising was likely, if not inevitable.

Mary Tighe's poetry developed at this point in the late 1790s when the sonnet 'Written in Autumn' was composed, perhaps because she was entering into her maturity both as a young woman and as a poet. She projects herself into the autumn landscape that lies before her and sees reflected there the changes to which her own heart and mind have lately been subjected: the death of a childhood friend at home in Ireland, the suspicion that she had consumption, the failure of her young husband to settle to any career and his diminishing love for her. As well as experiencing all these distracting misfortunes, she knew that she had brought some of them upon herself. There were opportunities for happiness which she had not seized and they had slipped out of reach. The poem is about the passing of time and acceptance of mortality:

> *O Autumn! How I love thy pensive air,*
> *Thy yellow garb, thy visage sad and dun!*
> *When from the misty east the labouring Sun*
> *Bursts through thy fogs, that gathering round him, dare*
> *Obscure his beams, which though enfeebled, dart*
> *On the cold, dewy plains, a lustre bright:*
> *But chief the sounds of thy reft woods delight:*
> *Their deep, low murmurs to my soul impart*
> *A solemn stillness while they seem to speak*
> *Of Spring, of Summer, now forever past,*
> *Of drear, approaching Winter, and the blast*
> *Which shall e'er long their soothing quiet break:*
> *Here, when for faded joys my heaving breast*
> *Throbs with vague pangs, here will I love to rest.*[11]

The advent of autumn mirrors the sense of change coming slowly over the earth and over Mary's life, which is moving slowly but surely across a watershed. The power of the sonnet as a whole springs from the third line, 'When from the misty east . . .' which moves in one long sentence to the end of the final line. Her skills in prosody, in all the arts of writing poetry, are already honed for the task of writing 'Psyche; or, The Legend of Love',which was probably started about 1800 or perhaps 1799 but certainly after the Rebellion of 1798. Some of the worst fighting took place in Wexford, not very far from the Tighe homes in counties Wicklow and Kilkenny.

By July 1797 they had returned to Rossana and Mary wrote with a lift in her voice of the beauties of the little River Vartry, which winds its way from the garden of Rossana Cottage, where she and Harry had spent several summers, down to the open spaces of the meadows around Rossana, and she reminds herself why she should stay here in the peace of the Wicklow countryside:

> *Here, Mary, rest! The dangerous path forsake*
> *Where folly lures thee, and where vice ensnares,*
> *Thine innocence and peace no longer stake*
> *Nor barter solid good for brilliant cares.*
> *Here woo the Muses in the scenes they love;*
> *Let science near thee take her patient stand:*
> *Each weak regret for gayer hours reprove,*
> *And yield thy soul to Reason's calm command.*[12]

Mary Tighe did 'woo the Muses' in the calm repose of Rossana but before she could commit pen to paper events intervened: the 1798 Rebellion reared its head right on the Tighe doorstep in County Wicklow and forced the family to decide where they stood. And William Tighe came back into their lives.

NOTES

1  Letter: Mary Tighe to her mother and mother-in-law, March 1794: PRONI 2685.
2  ibid.
3  Letter from Mary Tighe quoted by Caroline Hamilton: NLI 4810.
4  Journal of Mary Tighe: NLI 4810.
5  Sonnet: 'To Death', 1795.
6  Letter from Mary Tighe to Sarah Tighe, July 1796: PRONI 2685.
7  'Sonnet: 'Written at Scarborough', August 1796.
8  Letter from Mary Tighe to Sarah Tighe, Swansey [sic] September 1796: PRONI 2685.
9  ibid.
10  ibid.
11  Sonnet: 'Written in Autumn', late 1790s.
12  'The Vartree', July 1797.

# CHAPTER 7

# THE 1798 REBELLION
## *In the Hills of Wicklow*

*Billy Byrne of Ballymanus was a man of high renown,*
*He was tried and hanged in Wicklow as a traitor to the Crown;*
*He was taken in Dublin City and brought to Wicklow jail,*
*And, to our great misfortune, for him they'd take no bail.*

SONG (TRADITIONAL)

The 1790s have been termed the critical decade in the evolution of modern Ireland. The Rebellion of 1798 brought wild moments of hope for some and of deep regret for others as blood was spilled across the country. Stories of combat and heroism were moving and disturbing, for they cut across traditional allegiances. Harry Tighe fought for the Protestant Ascendancy as an officer of the Yeomanry, while his wife Mary gave shelter to a Catholic man wanted for the murder of local workers.

They had lived since their marriage in 1793 for the main part in England and Wales, travelling around the country but not often returning to Ireland. Dublin still looked elegant, perhaps more so than London. The pleasant squares, the leafy suburbs were arranged with an orderly charm that could not fail to please and the very grandeur seemed to suggest an affluence that could not be destroyed. In early 1798 they rattled up the road from London to Holyhead and decided there was no time to call in at Llangollen to visit Sarah Ponsonby and Lady Eleanor Butler, as they sometimes did, but they must go as fast as they could to Holyhead and take the earliest ferry. This journey in the late eighteenth century was often a gruelling experience, with long waits for passengers to make a full complement for sailing and delays caused by bad weather. The Tighes had the additional unhappiness of remembering Thomas Fortescue's still mysterious death just two days after his crossing of the Irish Sea. They were for once in agreement with one another as to what they should do: they must return to Rossana.

In the 1798 Rebellion in Ireland perhaps 30,000 people were killed in a few months. It was an unprecedented uprising and as significant in Irish history as Cromwell's incursions, the Jacobite wars and the Great Famine. One of the outcomes was the Union with Britain on terms which turned out to be unacceptable to the majority of the Irish population, since Catholic emancipation, which had been an implicit part of the arrangement, was abandoned. Such a settlement brought not peace, but a kind of fermenting pot of resentment and anger which would erupt in the Easter Rising of 1916, and lingers even to this day. The Rebellion took place because there was no British policy for Ireland. Pitt knew that the situation was explosive, that the ruling Protestant class and the Viceroy were fearful of subversive activity, that the Irish peasantry were very poor and likely to rise, but he was preoccupied with the war with France and unable to tackle the problem, particularly since the King objected to any consideration of Catholic emancipation and could not be persuaded to discuss the matter. Some anti-Catholic laws had been removed by legislation in 1778, 1782 and in 1793 allowing Catholics to inherit and purchase land, take a degree in university, become lawyers or hold public office, though the political power still lay with the Protestant Ascendancy and in fact this legislation benefited only a tiny proportion of the Catholic population – which would almost double between 1770 and 1800.

In 1782 the British government had accepted demands for greater independence and from then until 1801 the Irish Parliament was to run its own affairs, though the Viceroy and Dublin Castle moderated all that was done. There was a greater degree of independence from Westminster than there had been before. The leading figure was Henry Grattan (1746–1820). Indeed the parliament was known as 'Grattan's Parliament', and his achievements were an inspiration to the more liberal Protestants. He was the son of a recorder of Dublin, educated at Trinity

College, a Westminster MP and a practising barrister. Both William and Harry knew Grattan in a personal as well as a professional capacity; they were influenced by him and all three would work together in the Irish Parliament from the late 1790s. It can be argued that Grattan's period of influence was only a token in the wider political scene: his parliament did not achieve any ground-breaking independence for Ireland, but rather satisfied the Ascendancy sense of vanity about being autonomous. It certainly did not stave off the 1798 Rebellion.

To return to Dublin was to be aware of the imminent possibility of insurgency. Everyone spoke of the matter. There was restlessness in the city. Secret societies had been formed through which dissent was channelled and they became a force to be reckoned with. The United Irishmen had been founded in late 1791 with the aim of embracing reforms for Catholic, Presbyterian and Protestants alike. Theobald Wolfe Tone, Thomas Russell, Henry Joy McCracken and William Drennan led the movement whose first aim was to reform and democratise the Irish Parliament. The population had grown and the stability of rural life was threatened. Taxation was intensely resented. Trade restrictions imposed by the British parliament hampered aspirations to develop, and the Irish felt they were, like the American colonies which had recently made their bid for independence, mere pawns in the hand of an imperial power that did not consider their true interests. Ireland watched and saw the possibility for freedom. Many of the Protestant families in Wicklow and Wexford were sympathetic to the aims of this movement and, up until the fighting actually started, several of the Anglo-Irish families of liberal persuasion would not have been sure on which side to fight. Wolfe Tone was a focus for their dissent. He was born in Dublin, educated at Trinity College and politically active as a student. He began his political career as an important and revitalising force in the Catholic Committee in the cause of Catholic rights.

The Society of United Irishmen wanted to see an equal representation of the Irish population in parliament – this was its aim, along with independence from English domination. But at some point the Society's main thrust was no longer just parliamentary reform, and it came to believe that revolution was the only way to achieve what it wanted. The Society was suppressed by the government in 1794 because it was seen to be in touch with France and to have radical tendencies, which indeed it did. Wolfe Tone, now a young lawyer, left for America but went on to France where in 1796 he raised enough forces – a French fleet carrying 14,000 men – to set sail for Bantry Bay under the command of General Hoche. Tone embarked on the flagship of the fleet, the aptly named *Indomitable*. It was said that there were not enough troops in and around Bantry to deal with an army of this size. Official opinion stated that Ireland would have fallen had the invasion got off to a good start, but the weather was fiercely rough and the fleet was split from the General's command. Having hovered within sight of the snowy mountains of Ireland awaiting the arrival of General Hoche, they were shocked to see the wind change and turn into a hurricane. The remains of the fleet limped back to France carrying a young Wolfe Tone, who was bitterly disappointed. What might have happened had this exploit been successful? Might there have been an Irish Republic at this early stage, with General Hoche at the helm, a fantasy entertained by John Stuart Mill in his work *Ireland and England* (1878). This was the beginning of a mounting impetus towards rebellion in Ireland that would culminate in 1798.

The Tighes heard about events such as the fleet at Bantry Bay with a surge of conflicting emotion. Was Wolfe Tone brave or merely foolhardy? How dangerous his ideas seemed to the young Tighes. Several of the United Irishmen in Dublin were young Ascendancy lawyers or MPs from backgrounds like their own, people who wanted the best for their country and had liberal ideas about how to achieve it. William McNevin and John Lawless came from amongst the best Dublin families and were respected Dublin doctors. John Chambers was the personal assistant of Grattan himself, John Sweetman was a Dublin brewer and Richard McCormick secretary of the Catholic Society. Arthur O'Connor became a prominent and powerful United Irishman and he was a nephew of Lord Longueville. The most illustrious of them all was Lord Edward Fitzgerald, son of Ireland's first nobleman and largest landowner, Lord Leinster. Other United Irishmen were the new rich, such as Oliver Bond, wool merchant, and Henry Jackson, ironmaster, who owned a factory powered by steam. The radical barrister Thomas Addis Emmet was perhaps the leading intellectual of the movement, together with Arthur O'Connor. They read Thomas Paine and applied the ideas they found in his writings to the Irish situation: it was not hard to do so – there were striking similarities – and soon the smoke of rebellion was in the air. But it was Lord Edward Fitzgerald who captured the hearts of the people, resigning his seat in the Irish Parliament in 1793 after a passionate tirade against the government. He left for Paris and when he returned, joined the United Irishmen. His hair was cropped in the revolutionary mode of the French Jacobins and he had married a beautiful French girl with whom he drove through the streets of Dublin. Fitzgerald embodied the revolutionary spirit of the times.

Harry and Mary Tighe returned to Ireland in early 1798. They went straight to Rossana without staying in Dublin to find out what was happening. By this time, despite government attempts to disarm the rebels, the United Irishmen were gathered in militias across the country. Lord Edward's army in Kildare was perhaps not as big as that of Billy Byrne of Ballymanus, a member of the long-dispossessed Catholic gentry who was one of the delegates of the Wicklow United Party. He had built up his men from the disaffected of County Wicklow and amongst his soldiers were workers from the Tighe estate at Rossana. They thought of themselves as a citizens' army and had 13,000 men divided into eleven regiments. More than a thousand guns were smuggled into Wicklow and about 10,000 pikes were made to arm the people. This lethal lance, mounted on a very long shaft, was made by local blacksmiths.

Should Harry throw in his lot with men such as these? When he got home, he knew at once where he belonged and that was with the Yeomanry, the government troops who would eventually put down the rebellion. By 1796, the Yeomanry Corps had been set up to defend the nation against possible insurrection and by 1798 it had about 40,000 members. The Yeomans drew on the spirit of the Volunteers founded two decades before and they were mainly but not exclusively Protestants determined to protect 'their' country and vested interest and, as such, were seen by the radicals as a sinister source of further domination. Nervousness was everywhere and, despite efforts to increase the discipline of these men and to import arms for them to bear, there was an alarming sense of impending disaster. All over Ireland unruly forces, such as the Wicklow army, were awaiting their orders to fight. The government had tried through brutal means of torture, flogging and hanging to disarm the counties and as well as this they had managed to capture the wayward Lord Edward Fitzgerald on 19 May 1798, when he was betrayed by a double-dealing government official. But nonetheless, the uprising began on 23 and 24 May in counties Meath, Dublin and Kildare and spread through the next four months across the land. To the Tighe family, the horrors of the rebellion in Wicklow and Wexford were the most frightening experience of their lives.

Everyone they knew was involved and felt that their way of life was about to collapse. Some claim that the United Party in Wexford was very strong and they captured Wexford town and founded what is sometimes called The Wexford Republic, but there may be some exaggeration in this account. The influence of the United Irishmen has been overstated by later generations anxious to claim Republican achievement, and contemporary historians suggest that the leadership of the Rebellion was a complex mixture of Protestant landlords, wealthy farmers, priests and old Catholic gentry. One such leader was Bagenal Harvey of Bargay Castle, Co. Wexford, who was of the landed gentry. He fought alongside the young Catholic gentry of Wicklow, the farmers, traders, artisans, small farmers and labourers who made up the ranks of the fighting men. Their leaders were two Catholic priests, Father John Murphy and Father Michael Murphy, who fought with them to the end. When the government heard of the outrages at Wexford they sent General Sir John Moore to put matters right. He pushed into Wexford and routed the rebels. Each side committed atrocities and there was nothing to choose between them for ferocity. Not much farther south in New Ross, Co. Wexford, there was bloody fighting and 1,500 dead by the time the rebels finally took the town and the same day 125 men, women and children were massacred in a barn at a nearby village, Scullabogue, Co. Wexford – nearly all of them Protestants.

Some of the letters of the Tighe family written in 1798 tell of their experience of the Rebellion. Sarah Tighe, mistress of Rossana, knew exactly what was going on in her locality. How she must have welcomed the return of her son Harry, who arrived from England and immediately joined the Yeomanry. He kept her informed of events and Mary stayed with her at Rossana. Sarah's letters of this period vividly capture the family's experience. In April 1798, Sarah wrote to the Ladies of Llangollen of the prevailing atmosphere of mistrust in the community. Of the local men at Rossana and around County Wicklow, she said:

> . . . perhaps they think it prudent to become industrious and leave off whiskey. I think it possible the united business* may bring them into good habits for they carefully avoid getting drunk lest they should betray secrets. The English Government are wonderfully vigilant. They seem to know everything that passes in all the meeting, though whiskey is excluded. £4,000 has been subscribed in this county for such information, and some has been got, many stands of arms discovered.[1]

In the same year Wolfe Tone was captured at sea and committed suicide while awaiting trial. So died another young contemporary of the Tighes, a Protestant leader of the rebellion empowered by the Catholic French and fighting on behalf of the poor Catholic Irish, as well as his own peers who wished for greater autonomy in their own land. Lord Edward Fitzgerald was captured and wounded in a house in Dublin and died soon afterwards. Sarah Tighe wrote to the Ladies of Llangollen of his death:

> The vigilance of the yeomanry and the Government under God, has sheathed the daggers of the Assassins. It is hoped that the death of Lord Edward will keep them so and the great force that is in the kingdom and what they expect from England, will soon restore this country to peace. For the few years allotted to us in this world why cannot brothers live together in harmony?[2]

Sarah wrote to Miss Ponsonby of Llangollen on 21 April and sounded at first rather complacent about their safety when the fighting broke out. She was clearly as keen to reassure herself as much as the Lady of Llangollen:

* The United Irishmen secret societies.

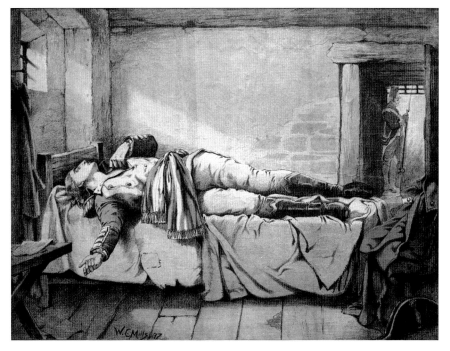

*The Death of Wolfe Tone by Walter C. Mills*

My ever dear friend,

Your last very kind letter deserves an immediate answer, the solicitude you express, my warmest gratitude. Nothing disagreeable, thank God, has happened to any of my family. We hear of wars and murders, but in this peaceful valley, we have no fears and continue unguarded, unfortified and unarmed. Many well behaved soldiers have been sent down to Wicklow and the adjoining towns under the charge of a very peaceable man, and our magistrates are all mild and sensible. The neighbourhood never was and I trust never will be as bad as the South of Ireland. The Dublin politicians tell us it is the design of the Roman Catholics to exterminate the Protestants.[3]

Later Sarah went on to chart the change of mood at Rossana as the rebels took charge of the fighting and, armed with pikes and much courage, nearly succeeded in overcoming the local yeomen who were supported by troops sent from England in response to the panicky demands of Dublin Castle. Between April and June the mood in the house changed to one of fear and the family decamped to the city. Sarah wrote again, this time from Dublin as 'the safest place', on 4 June 1798, convinced that the massacre of the French Protestants by Catholics in Paris and the provinces was about to be replicated in Ireland:

My dear friend,

In such perilous times, do you ever feel a perilous thought about Rossana and its present possessor? I will still hope you do and that it will give you some satisfaction to hear that she is alive and safe, and all her family, except Harry, who is perhaps at this moment engaged in the Wicklow Mountains and encompassed by a thousand pikes. He came for me last Tuesday, left me in town and immediately set out on a very hazardous expedition, God send him safe! We ought to be very thankful to the Almighty for having yet spared us, and that notwithstanding our many sins, we are yet well, though so many have perished in this cruel contest. I will not hurt your feelings by the relations I could give of private misery, when I tell you that the tragedy of 1641 is acting over again in this unhappy country. You may imagine, if you please, the various scenes now passing in the counties of Wicklow, Wexford and Carlow. I live in a state of suspense and terror. Not many days before I came here (as the safest place) a night like St Bartholomew's was fixed on. The vigilance of the yeomanry and the government, under God, has sheathed the daggers of the Assassins.[4]

For the time being, the Tighe family did not risk a return to Rossana and Mary waited anxiously for news of Harry. On 12 and 13 June (it took Sarah Tighe two days to complete her long letter to Sarah Ponsonby) she wrote, enclosing a copy of a letter she had received from a Mrs William Eccles of Wicklow about the Battle of Arklow, in which Harry was mentioned by name. Mrs Eccles's letter gives a vivid sketch of the extraordinary encounters of the 1798 Rebellion between well-armed British troops, Anglo-Irish yeomen and the pike-armed rebels, often led by priests who massed the troops in huge numbers and until the turning point at Vinegar Hill, outside Enniscorthy, Co. Wexford, seemed likely to win each encounter. But as Mrs Eccles's letter comments, the country men bearing the pikes who captured guns from their enemies did not know how to fire them.

About 7 yesterday evening came an express from Arklow, which threw this town into the utmost degree of consternation and alarm by bringing the intelligence of the rebels, to the amount of 20,000, having engaged the troops at Arklow. It is not in my power to give you the most faint idea of our situation here, this garrison greatly weakened, 100 men were all we had to depend on, had it pleased God to suffer the rebels to overcome our friends in Arklow and march on here. We were in the greatest despair and remained in that awful state of preparation for our last moment, when at about 11 o'clock we were almost struck dead by the dreadful shouts we heard at a distance and which seemed to be approaching nearer and nearer every moment and which we believed to be those of the rebels who generally approach in that manner…The battle lasted five hours and there was wonderful slaughter made by our cannon, while our troops received little injury from theirs. I heard one of the Ancient Britons say the appearance the enemy made was astonishing. They seemed to cover the face of the earth and carried their pikes so erect, they looked very formidable, advanced in a most regular order, each parish by itself and headed by a priest. One of them dressed with the insignia of their order, was shot directly through that part of his dress. Though the rebels were provided with artillery which they had taken at Wexford, they did not understand how to make use of them and obliged some of the men they had taken prisoner to fire the cannon, who aimed them so high, as to pass over the heads of their friends. All this good news would be nothing if at the same time, I had it not in my power to assure you that Mr Henry Tighe is well and in perfect safety.[5]

Henry Tighe had made a 'miraculous' escape, Mrs Eccles says, and the relief of the family to hear such news at Dominick Street in Dublin must have been profound:

20th June 1798, My dear Friend,

As you never had an account of our dear Harry's escape, I must mention it to you. The officers were supposed to be killed, belonging to the Antrim Militia, after Walpole through vile generalship had led the troops into the midst of the foe. Harry took the lead of fifteen Volunteers, and the rest, and had to cut his way through half a mile of pike men and back again, which he effected with only the loss of a few men. He distinguished himself very

*Piking the Loyalists on Wexford Bridge by George Cruickshank, 1798*

much, got great applause and has been pointed out as a person of great
bravery etc, etc. He is safe at Rathdrum and 'greatly beloved by his corps'.[6]

And Sarah wrote to 'Miss Ponsonby in Llangollen' on 10 June:

The plan pursued by the Government is to hem in the rebels in the
Co. Wexford and starve them into submission. Seven Generals have
encompassed them with their troops. Harry safe at Rathdrum though he
undergoes great fatigue by being sent on expresses (being Aide-de-Campe
[*sic*] to the Commander). It agrees with him very well.[7]

His mother put her finger on Harry's character in that she saw he had
discovered his first real sense of fulfilment while fighting. At last he had
found a sense of purpose. They had each found a place for themselves,
Harry in action with the Yeomanry, Mary in her sense of belonging to the
community, which she had so lacked in her travels up till now. They had
something important to share, she said: 'It was very interesting to hear
from Harry an account of the engagement he had been in. He seems to
pity the poor, who have been led into this war by designing gentlemen,
and ecclesiastics.'[8]

At this same time, Mary's brother John reported that the houses of the peasantry were burning in all directions near Altidore, Co. Wicklow. His fellow yeomen had shot many of the occupants as they ran from their homes, and he did not see anyone alive on his eight-mile ride that day. He could not explain why so many had been killed, except to say that the deed was done as revenge for the high number of loyalist funerals.

Harry's sympathies were for those on both sides of the conflict but they were not as complex as the feelings of his wife, whose naturally compassionate nature was drawn especially to the plight of the Irish peasantry, poor and vulnerable as they were. She brought into Rossana the Catholic man suspected of murdering workers on the estate. In the autumn of 1798 Mary wrote a ballad, 'Bryan Byrne of Glenmalure', that was published with *Psyche; and Other Poems* in 1811. It is about an incident that occurred when people who had worked side by side without thinking about their religious differences discovered that they were suddenly and mortally at war with one another. Twenty men were put to death near Wicklow in retaliation for the murder of loyalists, including the three brothers mentioned in Mary's ballad. It is clear that she knew and understood the spirit of resistance that informed the rebels' uprising, and equally she knew that her husband must fight in the Wicklow Mountains to subdue those who threatened the Tighe family inheritance. The conflict is reflected in the themes of her poem. She heard ballads sung by workers on the land, now realising that they were used to disseminate information about what was going on at the front and to create a sense of allegiance and devotion to the cause. She heard the workers at Rossana sing 'The Wearing of the Green'.

> *Oh Paddy dear, and did you hear, the news that's going round?*
> *The shamrock is by law forbid to grow on Irish ground,*
> *St Patrick's day no more we'll keep; his colour can't be seen,*
> *For there's a cruel law against the wearing of the green.*
> *I met with Napper Tandy and he took me by the hand*
> *And said, how's poor old Ireland and how now does she stand?*
> *She's the most distressful country that ever yet was seen*
> *And they're hanging men and women there for wearing of the green.*

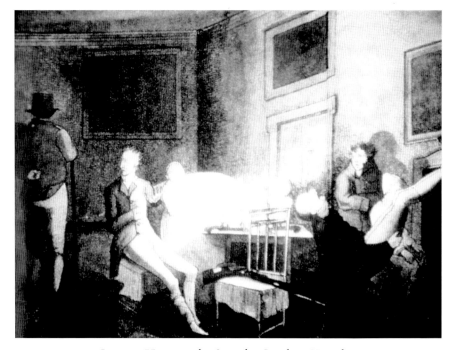

*Rossana House under Siege by Caroline Hamilton*

In September 1798, the Tighe mansion at Rossana was attacked. The purpose was to find arms. A rebel attempted to break in, but he was shot and wounded and further demands ignored. So the insurgents went on to the nearby estate of Ballynocken where they took Thomas, Joseph and James Byrne, two brothers and a son, who were all yeomen, and executed them. There was much publicity of this ruthless deed. Sarah Tighe's letter to her son William of 2 October 1798 tells of the incident described in Mary's poem:

> At Rossana: in the day we are comfortable, and forget that we are surrounded by enemies, when night approaches, our courage sinks. This house is now in such a state of defence, the soldiers say we could keep off hundreds, but unless a speedy change takes place, I should not think it right to stay. It appears, at present, as if my being here was useful. Many poor Protestants finding at night a safe retreat; from 20–30 come every night, and in the day the Roman Catholics are screened from the Military by being employed here. There were circumstances in the murder of the three Byrnes that have

raised a spirit of retaliation in the military and the attendant consequences have ensued. The chief aggressor in the massacre of the Byrnes was a R.C. whose life Mary saved by taking him into the house.[9]

In this tale of the three murdered brothers which is based on fact, Mary Tighe makes more than a glancing reference to the story of Billy Byrne, the rebel who fought bravely at the battles of 1798 as leader of the Wicklowmen. She sets the scene near her home as she writes: 'The autumn woods in Glenmalure/Look lovely in the slanting beam . . .'

She introduces a widowed mother, Ellen Byrne, who clasps a blue-eyed child to her breast. A horn is heard and she reassures her child that the sound is not the 'death-tongued bugle' with which he is familiar, but the hunting horn. A soldier amongst the huntsmen stops to enquire why the child is so afraid, 'Soldier, away, my father died,/Murdered by men of blood like you'. The boy flees down the glen, followed by his mother. The soldier asks who he is:

> *That boy had seen his father's blood,*
> *Had seen his murdered father's groan;*
> *And never more in playful mood*
> *With smiles his infant beauty shone.*[10]

He is told that the boy's father has been murdered in revenge for the death of three others who died locally.

Ellen's tale is told in the second part of the ballad and is of the three young yeomen 'butchered by savage treachery' on the Tighe-Ballynocken estate on 26 September 1798. In the ballad, the murdered boys are her nephews and she returns from discovering the bodies of the three young men to hear cries of revenge for their killing.

> *In throngs the assembled country came,*
> *And every hand was armed with death:*
> *Revenge! Revenge! They all exclaim,*
> *Spare no suspected traitor's breath.*

Ellen, her father and her son make their way back down the glen to their cottage and they are full of foreboding. They find 'the fiends scarce left their work of death'. Cruelly, Ellen's husband has been butchered in revenge for the deaths of her nephews. She is pulled apart by two tragedies. Her child clings to his dead father, 'And fast his little arms intwined/As round the bleeding neck he hung'.

Ellen's father cries,

> *Oh God, even now methinks I see*
> *My dying boy as there he stood,*
> *And sought with fond anxiety*
> *To hide his gushing wounds of blood.*

The family are enmeshed in both sides of the fighting, which hits them twice as the narrative pulls the killings together. The conflict is shown from both points of view and the poet asks the listener to consider whether any purpose is served by war. The ballad ends as the grandfather of the orphan boy and narrator of the tale turns to the soldier whose questions invoked the story of Bryan Byrne:

> *Soldier, farewell, to thee should power*
> *Commit the fate of lives obscure,*
> *Remember still in fury's hour*
> *The murdered youths of Glenmalure.*
>
> *And chief, if civil broils return*
> *If vengeance urge to waste, destroy;*
> *Ah! Pause! Think then on Bryan Byrne,*
> *Poor Ellen and her orphan boy.*

The orphan child is a victim of sectarian strife and the ballad is an eloquent plea for war to cease. Now Mary Tighe's poetry for the first time has a sense of prescience. For the modern reader it has contemporary resonance.

By August 1798 the worst was over but the Tighe family in Wicklow was suffering from the ill-effects on their health of the Rebellion. Harry had a sprain that prevented him from riding, his brother William had recurring attacks of asthma, Mary had been through a patch of general illness that was no doubt to be attributed to her consumption but made worse by the stressful nature of the times, and Sarah Tighe was suffering from general fearfulness and pains in the chest which she describes with characteristic dramatic flair in a letter to Sarah Ponsonby:

> I sometimes think seriously of trying to take a farm in the Vale of Gloucestershire, do you advise me to do so? I am afraid we shall be killed in the dark winter nights if we stay and poor little Susan is always starting out of her sleep at night thinking that a dagger or a pike is at her bosom. Some of us will die of apprehension and others of confinement. God send us better times and may He always bless you and dear Lady Eleanor, to whom I beg my best regards. The pain I get at the top of my chest is like the point of a Pike but when I cease to write it goes away.[11]

But eventually even Sarah Tighe's nerves were calmed. She decided the worst of the danger was past: 'It is impossible to guess the event or what will be the fate of Ireland. I am resolved to stay here and take my chance. The country is charming and I enjoy my farming affairs, as if there was no rebellion.'

As late as 1803 when Mary was immured in the attic at Rossana finishing the writing of *Selena*, the aftermath of the Rebellion rumbled on. The streets in which she had sat waiting in her carriage to go in to her first ball at Dublin Castle were now unsafe places. Mary thought she had sensed, even then, the pressure in the air. She heard from Thomas Moore the tale of Robert Emmet's attack on the Castle in July at the head of a hundred followers. A mob of citizens followed in his wake and committed various savage atrocities, including the murder of the Lord Chief Justice and his son-in-law who were killed with pikes as they sat in their coach. The insurrection was put down by government troops within a matter of hours. Emmet fled to the hills and rashly returned for a meeting with his lover, Sarah Curran, at Harold's Cross, only to be captured and hanged in Dublin on 20 September 1803. In 1807 Thomas Moore wrote his song in memory of Emmet:

> *Oh! breathe not his name – let it sleep in the shade,*
> *Where cold and unhonour'd, his relics are laid!*
> *Sad, silent and dark, be the tears that we shed,*
> *As the night-dew that falls on the grass o'er his head.*[12]

The younger Tighes went to London to see to their affairs, but they could not put Ireland from their minds: they were soon to return. There was no doubt any more for Mary about what she wanted to do. It was quite simple. It was time to write all day long.

NOTES

 1 Letter from Sarah Tighe at Rossana to Sarah Ponsonby, Llangollen, 21 April 1798, NLI 4813.
 2 Letter from Sarah Tighe to Eleanor Butler, Llangollen, 4 June 1798, NLI 4813.
 3 Letter from Sarah Tighe to Sarah Ponsonby, 21 April 1798, NLI 4813.
 4 Letter from Sarah Tighe to Sarah Ponsonby, 4 June 1798, NLI 4813.
 5 Letter from Sarah Tighe to Sarah Ponsonby, 10 June 1798, NLI 4813.
 6 Letter from Sarah Tighe to Sarah Ponsonby, 20 June 1798, NLI 4813.
 7 Letter from Sarah Tighe to Eleanor Butler, 16 June 1798, NLI 4813.
 8 Letter from Sarah Tighe to Eleanor Butler, 16 June 1798, NLI 4813.
 9 Letter from Sarah Tighe to William Tighe, 2 October 1798, NLI 4813.
10 'Bryan Byrne of Glenmalure', Autumn 1798.
11 Letter from Sarah Tighe to Sarah Ponsonby, 8 August 1798, NLI 4813.
12 Thomas Moore: 'Oh! breathe not his name', 20 September 1807.

# CHAPTER 8

# WRITING

## *'My first wild song'*

By 1801 Harry and Mary Tighe had changed the focus of their lives. No more the search for the thrill of the city, the constant journeying between fashionable towns in England, the quest for the ideal spa that might improve Mary's health. Despite the fact that the events of the 1798 Rebellion were still very much alive and the grievances which caused it were by no means resolved, they decided to make their permanent base in Ireland at Rossana. Mary retired to 'the bow room in the attic' which was on the top floor overlooking the River Vartry, the park and gardens of the estate. She looked out at the great chestnut trees, one of them said to be the oldest tree in the country and consecrated in public memory by the fact that it was the one under which John Wesley had preached. Here the sheer greenness of Ireland was at its best and quiet peacefulness comforted the poet after a life spent in rented houses in the so-called beauty spots of England.

Mary's Tighe cousins were settled in Ireland: Elizabeth Tighe married the Revd Thomas Kelly of Kellyville, near Athy, Co. Laois (Queen's County) in 1795 when she was twenty and soon had a family. The Revd Thomas Kelly was an evangelical preacher renowned for writing hymns, some of which are still sung today, such as 'The head that once was crowned with thorns'. Elizabeth's sister Caroline Tighe married Charles Hamilton in 1801 and went to live north of Dublin at Hamwood House, his family home near Dunboyne in County Meath and their first child was born the next year.

*Hamwood House, home of Charles and Caroline Hamilton*

Five more children followed. Caroline possessed the happy and successful gift of creating family life, as well as a sharp wit, and she painted many satirical sketches which comment on the social behaviour of the day. Mary was aware of her cousins' achievements and felt the need to define herself in a new way for it had become clear that she would not have children. Caroline and Mary wrote to each other up until the very last days of Mary's life. Their relationship was like that of sisters, but they were first cousins and 'in-laws' as well, since Mary had married her brother; the veins of family affection ran deep. Mary was attached to Caroline's children and to Elizabeth's as well. She was particularly fond of the 'little Kelly girls'.

A long time had passed since John Wesley had warned the young Mary at Gardiner's Row of 'idle books' that were not worth reading, particularly 'fine poetry'. In 1801 she was confident enough to know what she liked and to acknowledge her vocation. Two years later her poem 'Psyche; or, The Legend of Love' was 'copied out fair', 372 stanzas in all, each of nine lines. At the end of this period of work she would go on to finish her novel *Selena* in five volumes. Both were completed by the end of 1803. This was a precious period of her life in which Mary chose to make the most of such time as remained to her. Caroline describes her activity:

> As her health declined her love of occupation encreased [*sic*] and it was then she formed the plan of writing a long poem which she used to continue at intervals. In the same way and about the same time she wrote a novel, Selena, reading out to us the beginning and leaving us to guess how she meant to conclude it . . . When Psyche was concluded her husband admired it so much that he persuaded her to let him print fifty copies of it

to be distributed among her friends and as a few of them were given to the most distinguished characters of the day (C.Fox, Mr Hayley &c &c) her reputation for talents rose at once. She received many most complimentary letters and from that moment her society was eagerly sought for by all within reach of her who had any pretentions [*sic*] to literature or talents.[1]

'As her health declined her love of occupation encreased.' So wrote Caroline Hamilton with authority, aware of the disease from which her cousin suffered and full of fear on her behalf. From the seventeenth to the nineteenth century the major cities of Europe and of America suffered a tuberculosis epidemic of such vast proportion that it became known as the 'White Plague'. London and New York were particularly badly affected and the death-rate worldwide was estimated at seven million people a year, while fifty million were infected. Some even thought that the civilisation of Europe was under threat. It is a disease which can easily be caught and at this time at least half the world's population came in contact with it,

*The Gentleman Farmer by Caroline Hamilton.*
*The gentleman slouches at the fire, a dog licks up scraps from the table*
*and his wife yawns with boredom as the footman makes the tea.*

unaware of the fact that they could infect others. Mary Tighe probably gave the disease to her infant niece, one of the 'little Kelly girls'.

The list of literary figures and other artists who suffered from the disease is long and they would in the eighteenth and nineteenth centuries have termed their affliction phthisis or consumption. These writers and artists are often viewed romantically, as in the story of Puccini's opera *La Bohème* where Mimi is portrayed as a beautiful flower-girl who has left her poor husband as she hovers on the edges of sophisticated Parisian society. Her death in the arms of her lover is witnessed by the demi-monde of students and artists which she inhabits, and captures the tragedy of death from tuberculosis.

Because of the epidemic of TB in the period during which Mary Tighe wrote, there were many writers who could speak of their experiences of the disease and their wish to throw their last energies into a battle to overcome the despair of infection. We have as a result some highly articulate records of suffering. Some who were infected with consumption described being aware of a kind of dual personality, one passive, the other active and inspired. Keats wrote of this phenomenon: 'I feel more and more every day as my imagination strengthens that I do not live in this world alone, but in a thousand worlds.'[2] Charlotte Brontë wrote in her journal on Christmas Day 1848 of her sister Emily's 'strangely strong spirit' as she died of tuberculosis:

> Some sad comfort I take as I hear the wind blow and feel the cutting keenness of the frost, in knowing that the elements bring her no more suffering – their severity cannot reach her grave – her fever is quieted, her restlessness soothed, her deep hollow cough is hushed forever; we do not hear it in the night nor listen for it in the morning; we have not the conflict of the strangely strong spirit and the fragile frame before us – relentless conflict, never to be forgotten.[3]

The poet Francis Thompson (1859-1907) led his life in London as a tramp on the streets undoubtedly taking laudanum when he could get it to help him transcend the miserable reality of daily life. Despite ill-health and little security, he wrote poetry. The following poem, now a well-known hymn, was found unpublished amongst his papers at the time of his death in his forty-eighth year:

*O world invisible we view thee,*
*O world intangible we touch thee,*
*O world unknowable we know thee,*
*Inapprehensible, we clutch thee!*

*Does the fish soar to find the ocean,*
*The eagle plunge to find the air—*
*That we ask of the stars in motion*
*If they have rumour of thee there?*

The novelist D.H. Lawrence, who always claimed he had flu or a cold, refused to acknowledge his illness, but perhaps he transformed his own suffering into the energy with which he created Mellors, the gamekeeper of *Lady Chatterley's Lover*, which was written in the last stage of tuberculosis.

Because of such portrayals of people with the disease, attempts have been made to associate TB specifically with creativity, but they should be treated with caution.

> There seemed such a common association between tuberculosis and great art that the disease was invested with a specious romanticism and glamour. It was believed that tuberculosis could inspire genius, the so-called *spes phthisica* as if the bacterium infused the victims with some ambrosial stimulant.[4]

A unique causal link between creativity and TB based on a small sample of writers dissolves when seen among the millions of those who have died silently from TB across the globe. Such ideas do not take into account the fact that TB was one of the commonest causes of death in this period and the *majority* of those who suffered died undocumented deaths. A study of World Health Organization's Global Tuberculosis Report in 2012 puts such speculations into perspective and makes them seem unrealistic. The global burden of TB is huge: in 2011 there were an estimated 8.7 million cases of TB (13% co-infected with HIV). These deaths included 0.5 million among women worldwide. TB 'causes ill-health among millions of people each year and ranks as the second leading cause of death from an infectious disease worldwide, after the human immunodeficiency virus (HIV)'.[5] Progress is being made towards reducing the cases of TB globally; new cases of the disease are falling each year and the mortality rate has decreased by 41% since 1990, but it is still one of the top ten causes of death in all low- and middle-income countries.

However, there is certainly a link between creativity and illnesses of many different kinds. Thomas Mann said that disease is a means of acquiring knowledge and he studied tuberculosis in *The Magic Mountain* and syphilis in *Doctor Faustus*. The mind is concentrated by expected death and there is a special increased sensibility. The creativity of Van Gogh may well have been enhanced by his struggle with epilepsy, just as John Keats, with his knowledge of medicine, knew the precise significance of the scarlet arterial blood on his Hampstead pillow and made sure that his remaining time was fully used. Something of the kind can also be seen in contemporary society, for example in the art and literature of the early AIDS epidemic.

Mary Tighe's class, her family's wealth, her social status allowed her to make the most of her time. She was not ready to die and the years allowed her between her first symptoms and her death gave her will-power enough to write with remarkable speed and skill. Her health declined in 1801, and simultaneously, Caroline Hamilton says, she became busier, more ambitious. The product of this activity was a fine, very long epic about Cupid and Psyche which made her name in her day, her 'first wild song'.

'Psyche; or, The Legend of Love' opens with a sonnet addressed to the poet's mother:

> *Oh thou! Whose tender smile most partially*
> *Hath ever bless'd thy child: to thee belong*
> *The graces which adorn my first wild song,*
> *If aught of grace it knows.*[6]

Mary Tighe graciously acknowledges the influence of her mother upon her life – her knowledge, her learning. Less generously, Theodosia wrote of her daughter in her journal: 'In 1802 she forsook the Ballroom and Theatre, but was, perhaps not less misemployed in the pursuits of literature which she had never entirely neglected, nor were her literary companions less dreaded by me than her fashionable admirers.' The tensions of the relationship between the two are present in this entry, as is the fervent but narrow nature of Theodosia's religious belief. The very heart of Mary's being was given at this time to becoming a writer, yet her mother terms her 'misemployed'. Then Theodosia continues in a different vein as she expresses pride in her daughter's achievement: 'Her Psyche and Selena are monuments of her power and taste.' The word 'power' here suggests something of the shifting balance: Mary Tighe is about to write a poem which restates her own position as a woman.

The story of 'Psyche; or, The Legend of Love' was taken from *The Golden Ass* written by Apuleius in the second century AD. Mary Tighe closely follows her source for the first two cantos. This is a mythical tale of a king and queen who have three daughters. The two older women are fair, but the youngest, Psyche, attracts great attention for her special beauty. Her sisters make suitable marriages and settle down, but Psyche remains single and experiences no particular joy in being so beautiful. She is made unhappy by people coming to see her and to worship her. Such adulation of a mortal offends Venus deeply and she sends Cupid to avenge the slight to the gods. Cupid pauses in awe before the great beauty of Psyche and touches her with his arrow as she sleeps, but he accidentally grazes his own skin and, mutually wounded, the two are forever bound together. As far as her parents are concerned, Psyche is still unmarried and they decide to consult the oracle of Apollo at Miletus who commands that they prepare to sacrifice their daughter in a bridal funeral upon a great rock. The day for the funeral arrives and with great lamentation Psyche is led up to the mountainside which is her bridal pyre. However, just in time Cupid arranges for soft winds to bear her off to the Palace of Pleasure, where all is bridal bliss. They enjoy each other at last.

Soon Psyche's jealous sisters arrive to investigate her deified existence and learn from her that she is allowed to possess the delights of Cupid only so long as she does not see him in daylight – or in any light. The sisters counsel her not to trust men – particularly one who does not wish to be seen. How dubious is that, they ask? Psyche must set by her a lamp and a dagger and arise in the night to look at her sleeping partner, they say. Psyche does just as her sisters have ordered and stands over Cupid for a long while, rejoicing in his manly beauty, 'Speechless with awe, in transport strangely lost'. She is poised 'Between amazement, fear and ecstasy': but the god flees as he realises her transgression. She has broken her promise to him.

Thus far, it is not difficult to see why Mary Tighe was drawn to choose the myth of Psyche. Parental pressure upon young women to marry was only too familiar to her and she had experienced the sense of being admired and valued as a beautiful young Dublin socialite when what she desired was to be understood and known for what she was. Mary's tale now departs from the somewhat tedious Cinderella-tasks of sorting grain described by Apuleius, to which Psyche is condemned, and the next four cantos of her poem take us on a long allegorical journey in search of the god of love. It is a journey narrated in the manner of Spenser's 'The Faerie Queene' but with a more straightforward and inspiring message, for Psyche is led through trials of an extreme kind in which she changes and adapts her knowledge of the world as she gains experience, so as to emerge wiser and more certain of love at the end. She has taken her destiny into her own hands without sacrificing her beloved Cupid, though for almost the entire journey she believes he is lost. Mary 'Psyche' Tighe has now been created out of the ashes of the former timid, unformed female self who struggled in early years to find a path free of family obligations and pressures to conform.

And as a writer, she has found her own voice. Mary Tighe places herself in the literary canon and to do so she must compete with the masters of the craft. The demands of the Spenserian stanza are legendary: nine lines to the verse, a limited rhyme scheme of three, the last line, the alexandrine, having an unexpected extra strong beat. She manages elegantly, effortlessly; the reader never hears the cogs turning in the poetic mechanism, but pauses rather to admire a turn of phrase, a sound reflected in meaning, an unexpected inversion of the beat for emphasis. Mary Tighe was a key figure in the renewal of interest in this form, which her contemporaries Anna Seward and Mary Robinson had also employed. During the early part of the nineteenth century and a few years later others were to follow her: Byron was to write 'Childe Harold's Pilgrimage', published in 1812, Shelley 'The Revolt of Islam' in 1817, and Keats 'The Eve of St Agnes' in 1820 – all three were written in the Spenserian stanza, and there were many others.

From Canto 3 of 'Psyche' Mary digresses from the source of her story in Apuleius and converts the tale for her own use. The choice of allegory as the literary form provides an opportunity to explore familiar problems within the framework of imaginative disguise. To find the meaning of her tale is as much a quest as the tale is of quest itself. She wants her reader to be engaged in interpretation and discovery of what it is to be responsible for the soul. What does it mean to find the one you love? How can a woman achieve this state? Up to this point in literary time, the epic centred on the coming to maturity of a male, but in Mary Tighe's 'Psyche' the central figure is a woman. The more she experiences and endures, the more illuminating will be her enlightenment when the poem comes to its conclusion. And the writing of the poem is, like playing the harp, therapeutic for the artist.

Psyche has betrayed her lover: she has broken her promise never to see him except in the darkness of the night and has brought a lamp, as advised

*Drawing from a Bodleian Library copy of* 'Psyche; or, The Legend of Love'

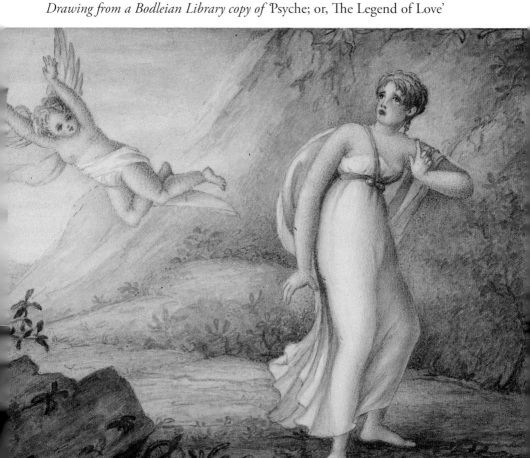

by her sisters, so that she can check that the mysterious nocturnal visitor is no villain set to trap her into a miserable marriage. But Cupid wakes as she views him and she is banished from his presence for her transgression. The wrath of the gods is incurred. Psyche must set out on a journey into the world alone, that is except for the 'stranger knight' who arrives to protect her in the forests and wildernesses she will have to traverse. This knight is refulgent in his strength and medieval readiness for battle:

> *In shining armour was the youth arrayed,*
> *And on his shield a bleeding heart he bore,*
> *His lofty crest light plumes of azure shade,*
> *There shone a wounded dragon bathed in gore,*
> *And bright with silver beamed the silken scarf he wore.*[7]

Mary's attention to poetic diction is always skilful. The sibilants in the words 'shield', 'crest', 'shade', 'shone', 'silver', 'silken', 'scarf' suggest the knight's crisp readiness to perform. And the last line of the stanza, an alexandrine, is longer than the rest, bringing the stanza to a rounded conclusion.

The knight too is 'divided from his love' and is as uncertain about what life still has to offer, as is Psyche. So their journey is to be undertaken side by side with the assistance of Constance, 'a beauteous boy' who seems scarce old enough to hold the bridle of the knight's milk white horse. A lion rushes from the forest:

> *A golden chain about his neck he bore*
> *Which richly glowing with carbuncles blushed,*
> *While his fierce eyeballs fiery rage had flushed . . .*[8]

This is Passion, the lion that roves at large in the forest into which they are about to step:

> *But scarce the kingly beast the knight beheld,*
> *When crouching low, submissive at his feet,*
> *His wrath extinguished and his valour quelled,*
> *He seemed with reverence and obeisance sweet*
> *Him as his long acknowledged lord to greet.*[9]

They proceed as a foursome, the knight, significantly, keeping the lion on a 'splendid chain with steady hand'. He can control the beast that is Passion and thus he makes Psyche feel sufficiently confident to get up in the saddle behind him. Her knight is never threatening in his behaviour and he always manages the dangers of the 'mazy wood' in such a way as to protect his 'fair'. Their passage is beset with difficulties. The 'Bower of Loose Delight', which seems to be populated with beautifully dressed guests, in fact holds terrifying serpents and when their veils are pulled back 'foul deformity and filth obscene' are revealed to the world. Like two young people at a social event in London or Dublin, Psyche and her knight arrive in innocence and leave in shocked understanding as they recognise the greed and depravity of the so-called guests. Constance keeps his eye on them both. Their journey through 'the mazy wood' is rough and alive with dangers but they press on to visit Vanity and Flattery, where the social scene seems to resemble a fashion manual:

> *Her braided tresses in profusion drest*
> *Circled with diadem, and nodding plumes,*
> *Sported their artful ringlets o'er her breast,*
> *And to the breezes gave their rich perfumes;*
> *Her cheek with tint of borrowed roses blooms . . .*[10]

Mary Tighe's exasperation and anger at the empty hours she herself had spent in such subservience is keenly felt here. Vanity and Flattery betray Psyche into the power of 'the haughty master' and she has to climb up the highest of mountains to the blazing castle on the peak, the castle that belongs to Ambition who invites her to sit beside him:

> *With cold indifference she looks on all*
> *The gilded trophies and the well-wrought stone*
> *Which in triumphal arches proudly shone:*
> *And, as she casts around her timid eye,*
> *Back to her knight her trembling heart is flown,*
> *And many an anxious wish and many a sigh*
> *Invokes his gallant arm protection to supply.*[11]

This picture of Psyche captured by Ambition, seated in his dazzling but ill-secured castle, asks for interpretation, as does much of the allegory – Mary herself has climbed these slopes. Frightened and aware of having been separated from her knight, Psyche glances back to him. Her trembling heart flies to him, to the man who has stood by her so stolidly throughout her quest. A terrible storm arises and Ambition's castle is not strong enough to stand against it: 'Down sinks the palace with its mighty lord'. The ending of this canto is happy, and Psyche's gallant knight slays Ambition.

The next canto begins with a passage of authorial comment in which we hear the voice of the narrator with whom we associate Mary herself. She comments on the near escape from Vanity and Ambition and reminds us that Psyche must not forget she is in fact on the quest for the immortal spring, the task set her by Venus when she first transgressed. Psyche must rely on the knight, Mary asserts. But despite this strong reminder, Psyche is betrayed by Suspicion into the power of Jealousy and left on her own to imagine her trusted knight in the arms of a lover:

> *Poured in soft dalliance at a lady's feet,*
> *In fondest rapture he appeared to lie . . .*[12]

But again, at the ultimate hour, the knight's soft voice resounds near her and she is rescued. At first neither can believe they are together again and find it hard to trust each other. The knight has 'withdrawn offended from her sight' (he can hardly be blamed for that). But reconciliation is at last achieved:

> *. . . Her soft lamenting voice has reached his ear,*
> *Where latent he had marked each precious tear;*
> *Sudden as thought behold him at her feet!*
> *Oh reconciling moment! Charm most dear!*
> *What feeling heart thy pleasures would repeat,*
> *Or wish thy dearly purchased bliss, however sweet?*[13]

Psyche has rejected the charms of living alone in a gothic tower, of being tempted by jealous thoughts and she is stronger for this, but the Palace of Chastity presents temptations of a special kind. The knight cannot enter here for he has been banished from Castabella's fair domain, 'For crimes my loyal heart had never known' and only after much pleading is he allowed in. In the Palace of Chastity, Prudence and Purity are handmaids and their tales enrapture Psyche. Songs are sung of famous women who rejected the advances of men – Daphne, Syrinx, Clusia, Lucretia, Virginia and many others, and now Psyche longs to join the 'white-robed, spotless choir'. The reader is asked to contemplate how easy it might be for someone to give in to the lure of Chastity, to retire completely from the temptations of the flesh in a way that could be seen as easier than living in the world. However, Psyche is released and she and the knight go back into the freedom of a sea journey lovingly described. Many dangers have been overcome – it seems that victory may be in sight:

> *Bright was the prospect which before them shone*
> *Gay danced the sun-beams o'er the trembling waves...*[14]

A terrible storm brews up and they are wrecked on the coast of Spleen. The knight tries to ward off Psyche's gloomy thoughts and they come across Patience, who receives and shelters them. She is a kind of female hermit such as only could be created by a poet of the early Romantic era:

> *Her head unshielded from the pitiless sky,*
> *Loose to the wild blast her tresses fly,*
> *Bare were her feet which prest the shelly shore*
> *With firm unshrinking step; while smilingly*
> *She eyes the dashing billows as they roar,*
> *And braves the boisterous storms so oft endured before.*[15]

Patience is determined to be patient at all costs, even at the price of life itself. She sounds a little like Mary's mother Theodosia, for her husband is lost. Many years ago his 'dear remembered bark' went off, never to return, though she still awaits him 'smilingly', her tresses flying in the wind.

They leave Patience to herself and at the opening of Canto 6 the young couple is becalmed. The lines that follow suggest the keenly felt power of Indifference. Mary Tighe undoubtedly wrote out of her own personal experience:

*Who can describe the hopeless silent pang*
*With which the gentle heart first marks her sway?*
*Eyes the sure progress of her icy fang*
*Resistless slowly fastening on her prey*
*See rapture's brilliant colours fade away.*
*And all the glow of beaming sympathy.*[16]

These lines depict her time in Scarborough in 1796 when she so resolutely remained outwardly cheerful but felt within her soul the pain of her failing relationship with Harry and the threat of mortal illness.

The treacherous slaves of Glacella (The Queen of Indifference and Selfishness) and her 'dark, ill-favoured lord' carry off Psyche: Glacella's castle, as the name suggests, is made of ice, and is in danger of melting. Psyche and her knight escape. At last it seems that the tests are drawing to a close for it has not been possible to part the two despite the most severe trials. Their voyage is concluded when they reach the Temple of Love: 'Love has home his Psyche brought'.

Psyche realises that her knight is Cupid himself in disguise, Cupid who has stood by her all the way and who has himself been on a soul-making journey.

*From his celestial brow the helmet fell,*
*In joy's full glow, unveiled his charms appear,*
*Beaming delight and love unspeakable,*
*While in one rapturous glance their mingling souls they tell.*[17]

It is only as the poem ends that the revelation is made: the true lover has just been recognised in time. He is the one who never gave up, who was also engaged in the quest, whose armour disguised his face. A physical and spiritual union follows in lines which are equal to any from John Keats's 'The Eve of St Agnes':

*Two tapers thus, with pure converging rays,*
*In momentary flash their beams unite . . .*[18]

The happy couple is invited to a blessing from Venus, who has forgiven all and she graciously deifies Psyche and the offspring who will be born of their union. Just before the final stanza, Mary Tighe speaks to those who have been less happy than Psyche and have parted from those they love.

Here can be heard the wounded voice of a young woman who has herself had to 'quit the object' of her 'tenderest love', returning to the reality of her own sad life:

> *Fond youth! Whom Fate hath summoned to depart,*
> *And quit the object of thy tenderest love,*
> *How oft in absence shall thy pensive heart*
> *Count the sad hours which must in exile move,*
> *And still their irksome weariness reprove;*
> *Distance with cruel weight but loads thy chain*
> *With every step which bids thee further rove,*
> *While thy reverted eye, with fruitless pain,*
> *Shall seek the trodden path its treasure to regain.*[19]

Mary has revealed her own values in the matter of love: the beloved is the person who stays until the end and does not fail; he is often hard to recognise, seeming simply to be a fellow passenger on the journey. The first in her own life to fulfil this description was John Blachford. Always attentive to her needs from her earliest years, her older brother had perhaps taken the place of her dead father. And her affection for her husband

*The drive at Rossana*

Harry had grown as she (and he) discovered what they wanted to do with their lives: he could claim the title of constant attendant. But behind the handsome head of Harry there shone another unvisored face, one which Mary realised had always been there, as far back as she could remember: the shining head of William Tighe. The cousin she had chosen to ignore. And what mattered most was that when William read this epic poem and reached the final lines he realised that he must make sure that Mary was not 'consigned to dark oblivion's silent tomb'. He knew and understood the significance of the Psyche story. Mary's work must be published and to achieve this end he knew that he must encourage her to get this done with Harry's help. The poem was what mattered now, because it was her acknowledgement of him. Mary Tighe understood he had been beside her in spirit on her peculiarly difficult journey through the mazy wood.

NOTES

1 Caroline Hamilton: *Mary Tighe*, NLI 4810.
2 Letter from John Keats to George Keats, 14 October 1818.
3 Journal of Charlotte Bronte, 25 December 1848.
4 Frank Ryan: *Tuberculosis: The Greatest Story Never Told*, published 1992.
5 *Global Tuberculosis Report 2012*, World Health Organization.
6 Sonnet: 'Addressed to my Mother', 1801-02.
7 'Psyche; or, The Legend of Love' written 1801-02, published 1805, Canto 3, lines 68-72.
8 Canto 3, lines 93-95.
9 Canto 3, lines 100-04.
10 Canto 3, lines 424-28.
11 Canto 3, lines 516-22.
12 Canto 4, lines 379-80.
13 Canto 4, lines 481-86.
14 Canto 5, lines 397-98.
15 Canto 5, lines 508-13.
16 Canto 6, lines 82-87.
17 Canto 6, lines 465-68.
18 Canto 6, lines 469-70.
19 Canto 6, lines 478-86.

# CHAPTER 9

# NEW FRIENDS

## *'Nightingales who keep watch'*

By 1803 Mary Tighe's novel *Selena* was complete, as well as her long poem 'Psyche; or, The Legend of Love' in which she had stated her belief in the importance of the quest for love and truth. Perhaps the effort of writing had exhausted her. In January 1804 she went to Dublin to join her mother, who wrote in her journal:

> . . . she brought a cough with her to town to which neither she or I paid sufficient attention, though on all other occasions I had been too anxious about her health – unavailing anxiety! – this sad cough never left her till it brought her to her grave six years afterwards.[1]

This condition had serious implications for her daughter's general health and Mary and a somewhat reluctant Harry made their way across the Irish Sea to England again, this time choosing to go to Bristol where the air reputedly was very pure and good for those with breathing difficulties. They would be able to visit the writer Hannah More, whose independent spirit was an inspiration to Mary and later in the summer they planned to return to London for an appointment with a talented doctor. His practice was flourishing and many people recommended him. Perhaps Dr Henry Vaughan would be able to find a way of halting the progress of her consumption. At least Mary felt that she was in charge of her own health, that she was taking some action to improve her situation of dependence upon her husband and mother.

However, right from the start their attempt to find new health for Mary in Bristol seemed doomed:

> We have been in our new lodgings about a fortnight and it is in the very first situation in Clifton and possesses the finest points of view of what is esteemed the finest air in the world, but alas! It brings no healing on its wings to me. I am not better, nor I fear shall I ever again know perfect health, but I hate complaints, remedies and would say, Physicians, had I not been restrained by the remembrance of Sol. Richards and the conviction that Dr Crawford (who however does me no good and condemns me to the torture of perpetual blisters) is a most amiable man.[2]

She acknowledged that she might never be truly well again and during the often sleepless nights at St Vincent's Rocks in Bristol she negotiated with herself about her own life, about how much time was left and what she might achieve. The Rocks were covered with woods that 'abound with nightingales who keep watch with us every night and sooth the painful hours of fatiguing exercises from my incessant cough and difficulty of breathing. I hear the little plaintive melodists as plain as if they were on my windowstool...' The choice of words says much: 'plaintive', 'plain'. In the homophones there is a sad and sonorous significance within which the word 'pain' is subsumed. It is hard not to think of the young Keats at Wentworth Place in London in May 1819 rising early and writing after a restless night's sleep of the nightingale that 'Singest of summer in full-throated ease'.

But the Tighes and Theodosia Blachford resolved to make the most of their days, even if the nights were difficult for Mary. Henry was despatched to London and mother and daughter decided to make a visit to Hannah More, who was a role model for independence of spirit. A single woman, she had bought land with views of the Mendips, the Bristol Channel and the Welsh hills beyond, and had built for herself and her sisters a two-storey house, Barley Wood, in which she was to live for most of the rest of her life.

> On Tuesday 1st, in consequence of an obliging letter from Hannah More, we paid her a visit of about two and a half hours at her very beautiful cottage among the Mendip Hills about twelve miles from this. The

cottage itself, the garden and its ornamental buildings vie in elegance of taste with Llangollen and though the surrounding scenery cannot boast of the romantic and wild sublimity of the Welsh fairy place, yet few spots in this kingdom can afford views of equal beauty (in the rich, cultivated style) with Barleywood, where Hannah More and her two sisters live.[3]

So wrote Mary Tighe to her cousin Caroline Hamilton in Ireland in June 1804. Hannah More, daughter of a Bristol schoolmaster and herself a schoolmistress for the first years of her working life, had become a familiar public figure as the author of plays, founder of Sunday Schools, writer of religious tracts and many other works. As a young woman she took every opportunity to spend time in London at the theatre and she became a great friend of the actor David Garrick and of his widow after he died. She socialised with Dr Johnson, with Horace Walpole and with the bluestockings of her day. Hannah More was a firm friend of William Wilberforce, whose crusade against slavery she supported. She had knowledge of the pleasures of life in London, of time spent in good conversation, of the thrill of meeting new minds.

She was a woman with many contradictory character traits and it was her ability to resolve conflicting ideas that appealed to Mary. She had earlier made a conscious decision to turn her mind and heart to a humble Christian life of charity when she moved to the Mendips. During the 1890s Hannah and her sister Patty founded a network of Sunday Schools in the region. The aim was not only to teach the children about the Bible but also to start reading-lessons for the children of the poor. Despite some initial difficulty in persuading the locals to part with their offspring, the schools were soon a flourishing concern and in fact one survived well into the twentieth century. William Wilberforce not only encouraged the More sisters, he also helped them with funding for the Sunday Schools. They had provided for the women of their local parishes by starting clubs for them, whereby for an insurance of a penny-halfpenny a week they could take sickness pay after childbirth. Dorothy Wordsworth started a school for poor children at about this time in Norfolk, as did Sarah Tighe at Rossana, and Theodosia Blachford had in 1802 founded the House of Refuge for unemployed and homeless young women on Baggot Street in Dublin. The women at Barley Wood in the summer of 1804 had much in common.

When they met in 1804 the gap of years between the two was considerable, for Mary Tighe was thirty-two and Hannah More was fifty-nine, more than old enough to be her mother. Volume III, Chapter 13 of *Selena* opens with an epigraph consisting of lines of poetry from More's play *Percy* – testimony of Mary's respect. Her long life of achievement as a single woman seemed to fascinate, as did the combination of worldliness and piety. Hannah lived in a cottage that had been purchased with money earned by her, for herself, and she was quite free to write as she chose. The three women walked round the house and garden and met the sisters and the servants. All seemed friendliness and warmth to Mary, who had seldom stayed anywhere in England long enough to feel at home. And this quiet cottage was clearly conducive to writing. Much of Hannah More's work had proved successful, from the publication of her early play *Percy*, written with the encouragement and advice of David Garrick and performed at the Covent Garden Theatre, to the 'Cheap Repository Tracts' commissoned to reform the living conditions of the poor, which she edited between 1795 and 1798.

Another visitor left an account of the happiness of arriving at Barley Wood, an account that she later passed to her great-nephew, E.M.Forster. The writer is Marianne Thornton and she remembers her childhood visits:

> Surely there never was such a house, so full of intellect and piety and active benevolence. They lived in such uninterrupted harmony with each other … that young or old one felt oneself in a brighter and happier world …
> I can now imagine our arrival at the door covered with roses, and 'the Ladies' as they were always called, rushing out to cover us with kisses, and then take us into the kitchen to exhibit us to Mary and Charles, the housemaid and the Coachman, then running themselves to fetch the tea things, Mrs Betty letting no one but herself to fry the eggs for 'the darling', the brown loaf brought out, the colour of a mahogany table, baked only once a week, of

*Hannah More by John Opie*

enormous size, but excellent taste . . . the peas we were set to pick . . .[4]

To arrive here in the morning after a night awake listening to the nightingales was for Mary an easeful release from thinking of herself. Her health was the first topic for discussion on her arrival with her mother because by now the symptoms of the disease that possessed her were evident in her face. Solicitous enquiries took place even as the visitors exclaimed at the beauty of the view and the charm of the cottage with its thatched roof and balcony running round at first-floor level. She received 'the kindest looks I ever had from a pair of lively, searching black eyes'. It is not difficult to imagine the somewhat stolid, capable, resolutely cheerful hostess looking hard at Mary and assessing her health, her character, her place in the world. But Mary, too, was watching Hannah More: '…yet in her manners there was an air of protection (as the French call it) and a consciousness of superiority which (though it never offends me) I am quite sensible is not, in itself, such as is best calculated to gain general love.'[5] By 'protection' Mary meant patronage; there is ambivalence in her response – she was fascinated by Hannah More's combination of a grand manner and a supercilious air with genuine sensitivity and kindness. She possessed a worldliness to which Mary did not aspire. Their portraits show a clear contrast between the straight, black-eyed gaze of Hannah, who stares thoughtfully and without self-consciousness from Opie's canvas while Mary's soulful yet equally thoughtful glance is turned away to some inward horizon with much more consciousness of self.

As she enquired about her visitor's health, Hannah asked about the relief of pain for she herself had often been prescribed opium. Such prescriptions were common at this period sometimes as a remedy for a specific illness and at others as a relief for stress of a more general kind. Coleridge had visited Barley Wood and the ladies had noted his shaking hands. Mary felt she could discuss such matters with Hannah and thereafter the visit was given to happy conversation. Theodosia could not sit quietly without mentioning the visits of the Wesley brothers to Rossana. She was pleased that her daughter was so impressed by this pious and influential woman; her continued and reiterated criticism of Mary's 'worldly' life in London found approval with Hannah, who in 1798 had written to Elizabeth Bouverie, one of a group of philanthropists from Teston in Kent, of her dismay at London social life:

> I saw so much of the shocking way of going on in the short time I was in town, that I *must* acquit myself to my conscience on this momentous subject before I die, if it please God. Dancing and music fill up the whole of life, and every *Miss* of fashion has *three* dancing, and a still greater number of music masters.[6]

Hannah More had held such views on the frivolity of life in the cities for many years now: she had called for a 'revolution in manners . . . a radical change in the moral behaviour of the nation' when she wrote *An Estimate of the Religion of the Fashionable World*. And in 1799 Hannah had published her *Strictures on the Modern System of Female Education*, in which, although she recognised the subordinate position of women in society, she revealed that she did not by any means regard women as being without power. There are many contradictory features of this work: Hannah More suggests women should keep a modest retiring demeanour, yet she wants them actually to have a first-class education so that they can be taken seriously and she objects to girls being tied to their 'phrenzy of accomplishments'. Her conclusion is that 'as keepers of the domestic hearth women were also the moral guardians of the country'. How close to Theodosia Blachford's moral and religious beliefs Hannah More's ideas came! Theodosia recognised her as a kindred spirit. They could even discuss the woman whom Horace Walpole chose to call the 'hyena in petticoats', Mary Wollstonecraft. Hannah liked to be seen as the very antithesis of such a woman (though she knew everything about her) and, unlike her daughter, Theodosia refused to read Wollstonecraft's *The Vindication of the Rights of Woman*, published in 1792.

Did Wollstonecraft appeal? She acted upon various ideas which had been contemplated by Mary Tighe: she renounced Christianity and proposed an alternative belief in the 'perfectability' of the human race. But most of her ideas were too far outside Mary's experience to be acceptable. Wollstonecraft had a lover, a child outside wedlock and wrote and published as she wished. She settled later to a happy married life with William Godwin and, in bearing his child, Mary (later to be Mary Shelley), she died. In *The Vindication of the Rights of Woman* she proposed that women's education should be unequivocally equal to a man's and that their narrow role in society should be replaced by a more enlightened one, with open access to full opportunity in life. Mary Tighe was interested in this ideology for she too thought that women had to some extent connived at their own imprisonment within society, but her poor health and lack of conviction did not allow her to experiment and the Methodist culture of her mother's household did not encourage discussion of such matters.

Theodosia was a devout follower of Wesley; Hannah was not tolerant of Methodists as vicars in her schools, yet both women were Evangelicals. Mary Tighe's diary, with all its doubts and fears, is much less certain of faith:

> Spent a miserable morning. Gloomy thoughts oppressed me and I vainly sought for refuge in philosophy or my feeble attempts at devotion. How often in the gloom of my soul do I say how blest are they who sleep to wake no more! Oh my God! How often have I desired to be as the insensible dust and asked my Creator why I was called into existence if I have not the power of obeying his supreme will? Oh No. I feel that his Love is beyond my thoughts.[7]

The older women were both too sensitive to Mary's now urgent need for mental and physical health to wish to lead her down the road of religious discussion on such a fine day out as this, and the Tighe-Blachford carriage took two happy people back to the nightingales of St Vincent's Rocks in Clifton, Bristol in the summer of 1804.

Soon after they took lodgings in London, in rooms at 15 Welbeck Street which stood conveniently near the hub of London life. This house was just within walking distance of Curzon Street, Mayfair, where Dr Henry Vaughan had his surgery and saw his patients in pocket-book order.

A medical man used his pocket-book systematically: Dr Henry Vaughan's were pocket-shaped – long and slim, and each page had the date at the top, giving a month to each notebook. They are very much the doctor's appointment log, and behind the elegant, marbled paper of the cover (pink, yellow and green) lies the record of each consultation for every day of the year. Both men and women of the eighteenth century used them and they were chosen with as much care as diaries are selected today. But perhaps then they were more personal and indicative of character, for fashionable people would have them made to their own special requirements. One might have a section for house-keeping accounts, another showed fashion plates for inspiration, with reference

*A page of Dr Vaughan's appointments taken from his pocket-book* to the location of shops where the garments might be bought and plenty of pages would be left blank for the daily journal.

Dr Henry Vaughan worked every day of the year, including Saturday and Sunday. He had no holiday from August 1804 to July 1805, the period for which Mary Tighe visited him. His patient list for Christmas Day, Tuesday 25 December 1804, when Mrs Blachford went round to his surgery, is full (perhaps Mary was too ill to go) as is the list for 1 January 1805 when Mrs H. Tighe consulted him. Vaughan's pocket-books show up to thirty appointments a day, which suggests that each patient had about fifteen minutes with him if he worked a seven- or eight hour day. And his list is flourishing in another sense in that it contains many of the famous names of the day. Vaughan could boast (and it seems he liked to) that he treated His Majesty, King George III, who sometimes appears beside Mrs Tighe, to Mr Pitt, the Duke and Duchess of Bedford, the Duke and Duchess of Gloucester, the Duke of Kent, the Duke of York, Lord Grey, Mr Canning, Mr Wilberforce, Warren Hastings, the Duke and Duchess of Devonshire, the Marquis of Lansdowne and the Earl of Westmorland. The Bishops of St Asaph, Cork, Lichfield, Winchester, Bristol, St David's and Durham, all of whom came to the consulting room at Curzon Street in Mayfair, provided excellent opportunities for conversation. The wide streets of a pleasant residential area allowed room for a number of carriages to draw up. Mrs Tighe usually had her appointment in the middle of the day; she was a part of that bustling queue and, as she joined the line to get her prescription, she made friends with those who returned week after week, which is part of the explanation of why she stayed for a year in London. A doctor could offer palliative care, he could give hope, but there were in fact very few cures indeed for any diseases.

Asked to assess the work of the eighteenth-century president of the Royal College of Physicians, Vaughan's Victorian biographer William Munk, wrote:

> Dr Vaughan's business even before his attendance on the Duchess of Devonshire was already very large and his professional income considerable.

*Dr Henry Vaughan, later Sir Henry Halford by Sir Thomas Lawrence*

In the year 1805, it had amounted to £7,700 and there were few families of station or note in England by one or two members of which he had not been consulted. His list of patients previous to this comprises a large number of persons of rank, and many eminent in politics and in all departments of public life.[8]

Towards the end of his career, Dr Vaughan renamed himself Sir Henry Halford. He had inherited the title from a relative and relished his new position in society.

The eighteenth-century painter Sir Thomas Lawrence, who portrayed the King and many people of the day, painted a fine portrait of Sir Henry Halford which hangs in the place of honour on the first floor of the Royal College of Physicians from where he gazes confidently at the viewer from his elegantly furnished room, his arms resting on the chair in an open gesture of greeting such as that with which he first met Mary Tighe on 23 August 1804. In the atrium of the modern building at Regent's Park he looks down at at the crowds of young doctors hurrying to their conferences about treatment with drugs he could never have imagined. His skill lay in caring, in communicating hope and in alleviating pain with the prescription of opiates. There is no doubt that his appeal for Mary Tighe lay partly in his social poise and position as physician to the upper classes, but she was also attracted by his ability to discuss the classics. He wrote poetry in Latin in his spare time. They discussed her work and her capacity for writing. How much was it sensible for her to attempt to do? As a consumptive patient, she had to use willpower to override feelings of fatigue and yet sometimes had unexpected and unexplained floods of creative energy. He put himself in touch with her, he helped her control pain so as to live with reasonable hope, while being realistic about her prospects of total recovery. He reached across the gulf of doubt and told her he could prolong her life a little. Munk wrote in his concluding chapter: 'He had too in a very marked degree, the power of fixing his attention on the subject before him, to the exclusion of other thought, or of distractions of any kind, and he habitually cultivated this faculty in all circumstances. Nothing is more important than this habit of fixed attention.'

So when Mary Tighe arrived in London in July 1804 fresh from her visit to Hannah More, she was ready to respond to the interest shown by her confident, eager physician whose sense of purpose in life contrasted so markedly with her husband's lack of direction. His worldly success, his ambition and good application provided her with a ruefully sad comparison to Henry, who worked for very few days of the year, if any, while this man worked all the hours he could in such a good cause.

Mary visited her doctor twenty-three times in the month of September 1804, almost every day. He had become someone she now felt she needed to see regularly and he was certainly a good friend and was becoming a little more than this. He was only six years older than her and on her birthday, 9 October 1804, when she visited him for her appointment, Mary brought her doctor a poem which she gave to him inside a collection of poems by Horace. It was addressed to him:

> *Yet well thou knowst, with gentler spell,*
> *To smooth the couch of pain and fear,*
> *The darkest shades with hope dispel,*
> *The oppress'd console, the languid cheer.*
>
> *Nor did the partial God deny*
> *The soothing charm of Eloquence,*
> *But bad its powers asswasive try*
> *To lull the pang-awaken'd sense.*
>
> *And thee with mildest manners blest*
> *Enlightened skill, and polish'd mind*
> *Our confidence secure to rest,*
> *Propitious fortune bad us find–*
>
> *What e'er thine art could do, is done,*
> *With each attentive, flattering care,*
> *And pleas'd, I proudly wish to own,*
> *A more than common interest there.*
>
> *That grateful on some future day,*
> *If skill at length have power to save,*
> *Delighted Memory may say,*
> *It was a **friend** these comforts gave!*[9]

Here in the consulting room she did not have to pretend that 'the darkest shades' never visited her, she could openly acknowledge her sadness. Her perception was too sharp to be able to delude herself and, without doubt, she had the measure of the man and knew she needed just such a physician to help her make the most of her last years. In the emphasised word *friend* can be heard the plaintive cry for a contact that rises above the merely professional, the need for an intellectual equal with whom she had rapport. Perhaps Vaughan filled the gap left by her father, for with the physician's power he could direct her life, advise her how to manage it and do so with firmness and affection. Or perhaps he – the other Henry in her life – was simply all that her husband Henry was not: a genuine intellectual companion and a powerful one at that. Among Vaughan's papers, now stored in the library of the Royal College of Physicians, thrown in with notes from his time at Medical School and notes on the deaths of eminent persons, lies a poem written by him about the value of friendship and snares of love:

> *Hence with thy meteor-fires, delusive love,*
> *Desire some other wretch, too well I know*
> *Too keen have felt the pangs thy tortures prove,*
> *Alive to every form of varied woe.*
>
> *Hence amorous Hope! No more thy arts beguile*
> *For other brows thy fading garlands twine,*
> *I turn disgusted from thy fatal smile,*
> *And all thy gaudy colours cease to shine.*
>
> *Sober friendship, who with constant light*
> *Shedst thy mild beams unknowing of decay,*
> *Unvexed by passion, uniformly bright*
> *Pour thy pure lustre on my devious way.*

But despite his pleas to friendship, the poem ends with an address to love:

> *Resistless God! Can ought thy wiles escape.*
> *Too late I see thy treacherous Arts confest*
> *Nor knew thee veil'd in Friendship's borrowed Hope*
> *To wing a surer arrow to my breast.*[10]

This poem is a subtle acknowledgement of the power of love. Vaughan knew how easily the goddess could veil her wiles in the guise of friendship and shoot an arrow more surely because she had taken aim.

There is no doubt but that Sir Henry Halford, as Henry Vaughan renamed himself, became a very sensitive and successful practitioner. He was criticised for opposing the physical examination of patients and for not keeping up with contemporary discoveries in pathology, which limited his diagnoses. He was considered unscientific by his more modern peers, some of whom felt that tact mattered to him more than curing his patients. However, he was one of the men called to care for King George III in his madness when he and Dr Baillie were the principal royal physicians, which is no uncertain tribute to his skills. Both these men believed that treatment of the insane should be made with unfailing kindness and not with violence, as was commonly the case at the time. They travelled down to Windsor to care for the King and from time to time took up residence there; Henry Halford was present at his death in 1820. It is also significant that he treated the King's daughter, Princes Amelia, who had 'consumption of the lungs' like Mary Tighe. Amelia had secretly married General Fitzroy and refused to reveal her secret. She had troubles of all kinds and the case called for delicate treatment. Sir Henry Halford appears to have gained her full confidence and her sympathy as well and in fact she asked Halford to be the go-between between the King and herself, a difficult task which he managed with discretion and understanding.

Mrs Theodosia Blachford appears several times in the appointments book. Perhaps she was summoned as Mary's mother to be quietly filled in on her daughter's state of health. Or had the strain of nursing Mary taken its toll? Did she herself require the doctor's services?

One patient is reported to have said she would prefer to die in Halford's care than to recover under any other physician. Mary Tighe did not have such a choice for her family wanted her to go back to Ireland, which she did in August 1805, but only after waiting until Dr Vaughan said she was well enough to manage the journey. She had benefited from her doctor's care and friendship, she had visited him regularly almost every day for nearly a year and she would have agreed with Samuel Taylor Coleridge who wrote in his *Table Talk*, 'In the treatment of nervous diseases he is the best physician who is the most ingenious inspirer of hope'.

Mary took home with her the best aspects of her relationship with her physician: a new confidence that she had life yet to live, revived faith in her own remarkable talents and courage and acceptance of the fact that Harry needed some freedom, just as she did. She had learnt about intellectual companionship and the blessings it confers. And she needed to return to Ireland to 'make her soul'.

NOTES

1 Theodosia Blachford: *Observations on the Journal of Mary Tighe*, NLI 4810.
2 Caroline Hamilton: *Mary Tighe*, NLI 4810.
3 ibid.
4 Anne Stott: *Hannah More, The First Victorian*, OUP 2003.
5 Caroline Hamilton: *Mary Tighe*, NLI 4810.
6 Letter to Elizabeth Bouverie, April 1798.
7 *Journal of Mary Tighe*, NLI 4810.
8 William Munk: *The Life of Sir Henry Halford*, Longmans, Green and Co, 1895.
9 'Verses addressed to Henry Vaughan', 9 October 1804.
10 Verses by Dr Henry Vaughan available in his archive at The Royal College of Physicians, Regent's Park, London.

# CHAPTER 10

# JOHN KEATS AND MARY TIGHE
## *'Thy plaintive anthem fades'*

M ary Tighe and John Keats never met, but her work was
undoubtedly an influence upon him and it is significant that
one of her sonnets was copied out and sent by the poet to
his brother George in America in 1818. The poem was included as John
Keats's *own* composition and passed unchallenged for a score of years in
H. Buxton Forman's 1883 edition *The Works of John Keats*. The fact that the
error remained undetected for so long suggests the extent of Keats's debt to
Mary Tighe. The title of Mary Tighe's sonnet is 'Addressed to my Brother,
1805' but Forman entitled the poem 'Sonnet: To George Keats':

> *Brother belov'd! if health shall smile again,*
> *Upon this wasted form and fever'd cheek;*
> *If e'er returning vigour bid these weak*
> *And languid limbs their gladsome strength regain;*
> *Well may thy brow the placid glow retain*
> *Of sweet content, and thy pleased eye may speak*
> *Thy conscious self applause: but should I seek*
> *To utter what this heart can feel, ah! vain*
> *Were the attempt! Yet kindest friends, as o'er*
> *My couch ye bend, and watch with tenderness*
> *The being whom your cares could e'en restore,*
> *From the cold grasp of death; say, can you guess*
> *The feelings which this lip can ne'er express?*
> *Feelings deep fix'd in grateful memory's store!*[1]

Forman's note on the sonnet runs as follows:

> This sonnet is from a transcript in the handwriting of George Keats, which bears the date 1819; but I am disposed to think this date must have been wrongly affixed from memory. The entire absence of high poetic feeling indicates a time of utter physical prostration; and I should imagine that the sonnet might possibly have been written in February, 1820, when Keats was so ill as to be forbidden to write, and that it might have been sent to George with the announcement of the illness; but it seems likelier that it was composed later on in the year, in reply to some letter written by George on receiving that news – a letter in which the younger brother might have reproached himself for leaving the elder, low in health and funds, and for rushing back to America to mend his own fortunes.[2]

*John Keats by Joseph Severn*

Forman's mistaken belief that John Keats wrote this poem arose from the fact that Keats and Mary Tighe suffered from the same symptoms – those of consumption. And both wrote letters to their brothers.

As a young poet, John Keats had been influenced by Mary Tighe. As he began to write, he would gather with his friend George Felton Mathew to read and learn from contemporary poets of the late eighteenth and early nineteenth century such as Charlotte Smith, Thomas Moore, Mary Robinson, William Hayley, Lord Byron, Leigh Hunt and Mary Tighe. The two friends wrote poems to each other experimenting with different forms and metrical arrangements which they copied out into commonplace books. There was much 'sentimental melancholy' for that was the fashion of the day. The writing of verse was a social activity for these poets, many of whom were very popular in their lifetime. Charlotte Smith's *Elegiac Sonnets* went through eleven editions from 1784 to 1800. There has recently been a revival of interest in her work and the same is the case for Mary Tighe.

John Keats first mentions Mary Tighe in an early poem written 'To Some Ladies, On Receiving a Curious Shell'. The ladies, who were the cousins of his friend George Felton Mathew, sent him a gift while on holiday by the sea:

> *If a cherub, on pinions of silver descending,*
> *Had brought me a gem from the fret-work of Heaven;*
> *And smiles, with his star-cheering voice sweetly blending,*
> *The blessings of Tighe had melodiously given;*
>
> *It had not created a warmer emotion*
> *Than the present, fair nymphs, I was blessed with from you;*
> *Than the shell, from the bright golden sands of the ocean*
> *Which the emerald waves at your feet kindly threw.*[3]

At the end of this poem, Forman notes of Keats: 'The reference to Mrs Tighe, the authoress of the now almost forgotten poem of "Psyche", is significant as an indication of the poet's taste in verse at this period.'

A fine example of his debt to her can be seen in the final stanza of 'Ode to a Nightingale' where the poet laments the fading of the song of the 'immortal bird' which had carried him on the wings of poetry away from the world where 'beauty cannot keep her lustrous eyes'. The concept and expression resemble the final stanza of Mary Tighe's 'Psyche; or, The Legend of Love' in the lines where the poet says her farewell to Fancy, or the power of imagination which has allowed her to create the story of Psyche's long journey to fulfilled happiness in love. The poet who narrated the tale for us takes leave of her imaginary world and descends to the 'silent tomb'. There is a powerful sense of disenchantment: the dreamer at the end of John Keats's 'Ode to a Nightingale' floats gently down to earth in much the same manner. For both poets, writing had the power of an intense reverie into which the poet retreated and to return to the real world was often an ordeal, one which was associated with the symptoms of tuberculosis from which they both suffered. Or perhaps for both John Keats and Mary Tighe, both of whom were treated with opium-based drugs, the endings of the poems quoted above delineate withdrawal.

MARY TIGHE (1802)

*Dreams of delight farewell! your charms no more*
*Shall gild the hours of solitary gloom!*
*The page remains – but can the page restore*
*The banished bowers which Fancy taught to*
  *bloom?*
*Ah no! her smiles no longer can illume*
*The path my Psyche treads no more for me;*
*Confined to dark oblivion's silent tomb*
*The visionary scenes no more I see,*
*Fast from the fading lines the vivid colours flee!*

JOHN KEATS (1819)

*Forlorn! the very word is like a bell*
  *To toll me back from thee to my sole self!*
*Adieu! the fancy cannot cheat so well*
  *As she is fam'd to do, deceiving elf.*
  *Adieu! adieu! Thy plaintive anthem fades*
    *Past the near meadows, over the still stream,*
    *Up the hill-side; and now 'tis buried deep*
    *In the next valley-glades:*
  *Was it a vision, or a waking dream?*
  *Fled is that music: – Do I wake or sleep?*[4]

As they conclude their works, the poets consider the power of the imagination to create a world in which the mind can live for a period of grace that will be ended by retreat to the darkness of everyday life, to the 'silent tomb' in Mary Tighe's lines and to burial 'in the next valley-glades' in Keats. The words 'vision' and 'visionary' in the final lines conclude the stanzas. Keats must have absorbed Mary's words at an unconscious level at least; they mesmerised his young mind and he was never entirely to shake off the enchantment.

Mary Tighe's influence is also to be detected in the subjects Keats chose in his early work. The poem in which the parallels of word and idea are most striking is 'The Eve of St Agnes'. Keats's heroine Madeline who languorously makes her way to bed and hopes to dream of her lover 'Upon the honey'd middle of the night' is much like Psyche lying on her couch awaiting the visitation of Cupid. The setting in the great medieval castle is vivid in Keats's poem:

> *A casement high and triple-arch'd there was,*
> *All garlanded with carven imag'ries*
> *Of fruits, and flowers, and bunches of knot-grass,*
> *And diamonded with panes of quaint device,*
> *Innumerable of stains and splendid dyes,*
> *As are the tiger-moth's deep-damsk'd wings;*
> *And in the midst, 'mong thousand heraldries,*
> *And twilight saints, and dim emblazonings,*
> *A shielded scutcheon blush'd with blood of queens and kings.*[5]

And, by comparison, Psyche enters the Palace of Love:

> *Increasing wonder fill'd her ravish'd soul,*
> *For now the pompous portals open'd wide,*
> *There pausing oft, with timid foot she stole*
> *Through halls high-dom'd, enrich'd with sculptur'd pride,*
> *While gay saloons appear'd on either side*
> *In splendid vista opening to her sight;*
> *And all with precious gems so beautified,*
> *And furnish'd with such exquisite delight,*
> *That scarce the beams of heaven emit such lustre bright.*[6]

In each there is to be music and a feast of Eastern delicacies as the lovers come to know each other. The revelation of identity and the consummation of love in 'The Eve of St Agnes' and 'Psyche; or, The Legend of Love' is strikingly similar:

> *Scarce on the altar had she placed the urn,*
> *When lo! in whispers to her ravished ear*
> *Speaks the soft voice of Love! 'Turn, Psyche, turn!*
> *And see at last, released from every fear,*
> *Thy spouse, thy faithful knight, thy lover here!'*
> *From his celestial brow the helmet fell,*
> *In joy's full glow, unveiled his charms appear,*
> *Beaming delight and love unspeakable,*
> *While in one rapturous glance their mingling souls they tell.*
>
> *Two tapers thus, with pure converging rays,*
> *In momentary flash their beams unite,*
> *Shedding but one inseparable blaze*
> *Of blended radiance and effulgence bright,*
> *Self-lost in intermingling light;*
> *Thus in her lover's circling arms embraced,*
> *The fainting Psyche's soul, by sudden flight,*
> *With his its subtlest essence interlaced;*
> *Oh! bliss too vast for thought! By words how poorly traced!*[7]

The mingling of the lovers in 'one inseparable blaze' is a complex conceit which Mary Tighe uses to suggest the loss of self and the radiance of Psyche's assumption into the realm of the gods as she embraces Cupid, her true love. Keats's lovers, Porphyro and Madeline, blend into one another in an equally sensual image:

> *Beyond a mortal man impassion'd far*
> *At these voluptuous accents, he arose,*
> *Ethereal, flush'd, and like a throbbing star*
> *Seen mid the sapphire heaven's deep repose;*
> *Into her dream he melted, as the rose*
> *Blendeth its odour with the violet,–*
> *Solution sweet: meantime the frost-wind blows*
> *Like Love's alarum pattering the sharp sleet*
> *Against the window-panes; St Agnes' moon hath set.*[8]

The language of Mary Tighe was absorbed into Keats's very blood. But what is most often remembered of John Keats's relationship with Mary Tighe is that he dismissed her as an influence when in an important letter of December 1818, he wrote to his brother George in America: 'Mrs Tighe and Beattie once delighted me – now I see through them and can find nothing in them but weakness, and yet how many they still delight.' James Beattie, Professor of Moral Philosophy at Aberdeen University and also a poet who wrote 'The Minstrel' in Spenserian stanzas, fell from Keats's favour suddenly, in the same manner. The question is: why did Keats feel the need to reject her influence upon his work? The answer lies partly in his still undeveloped ability to understand the women in his life and partly in his development as a poet. He perhaps found it easier to think of his role models as male and he was to move on from his own early style, from his 'Spenserian' stage, and come into full throat for his *annus mirabilis* 1819, the year in which he wrote the Odes. In the following quotation from his letters, Keats considers how thoughts change as knowledge is accumulated. A young man's ideas expand, are modified, augmented, rejected and replaced as new reading and experience determine what he thinks. He continues with thoughts about his changing taste in art:

A year ago I could not understand in the slightest degree Raphael's cartoons – now I begin to read them a little. We with our bodily eyes see but the fashion and Manners of one country for one age – and then we die. Now to me manners and customs long since passed whether among the Babylonians or the Bactrians are as real, or even more real than those among which I now live – My thoughts have turned lately this way – The more we know the more inadequacy we find in the world to satisfy us – this is an old observation; but I have made up my Mind never to take anything for granted – but even to examine the truth of the commonest proverbs.[9]

Keats needs to find his own voice in order to express his most mature ideas, reading, reflecting, watching the world, rejecting some, adopting new writers. But sadly for Mary Tighe's reputation, the lines about Keats's rejection of her have become better known in the modern age than her poetry. Despite the many editions of 'Psyche; or, The Legend of Love' that were printed in the first half of the nineteenth century, there has never been a complete edition of her collected poems in Ireland or Britain, though there is an American edition.

Keats acknowledges Spenser rather than Mary Tighe:

> *Spenser! A jealous honourer of thine,*
> *A forester deep in thy midmost trees,*
> *Did, last eve, ask my promise to refine*
> *Some English, that might strive thine ear to please.*[10]

Wordsworth, Coleridge and Byron all used the Spenserian stanza. John Keats and Mary Tighe were both fascinated by Spenser's theme of mutability versus eternity, one which many poets of the period took up. Keats moved on to other forms. In April 1819 he wrote a poem with the title 'Ode to Psyche' which in many ways reads as a reference to Mary Tighe's *magnum opus*.

At the opening of 'Psyche; or, The Legend of Love', Psyche, or the soul, undergoes many trials before she is united with Cupid and joins with him in celestial nuptial bliss. Keats's 'Ode to Psyche' begins where Tighe ends with Psyche and Cupid kneeling in the grass in happy union:

> *They lay calm-breathing on the bedded grass;*
> *Their arms embraced and their pinions too;*[11]

Keats says that Psyche has joined the pantheon of gods later than most. She has,

> *No shrine, no grove, no oracle, no heat*
> *Of pale-mouth'd prophet dreaming.*

The poet himself will be her priest:

> *Yes, I will be thy priest, and build a fane\**
> *In some untrodden region of my mind,*
> *Where branched thoughts, new grown with pleasant pain,*
> *Instead of pines shall murmur in the wind:*

Within this sanctuary, Keats will worship Psyche, or the soul:

> *And there shall be for thee all soft delight*
> *That shadowy thought can win,*
> *A bright torch, and a casement ope at night,*
> *To let the warm Love in!*

This is clearly an important statement of his intention to open the whole of his being to the quest for love and the expression of his ideas through poetry. How similar this quest is to that of Mary Tighe's Psyche. She was a source of inspiration to Keats as a very young man and was one of the stepping stones in his path to a mature poetic voice.

Keats knew that Shakespeare had used the word 'darkling' and he used it in 'Ode to a Nightingale':

> *Darkling I listen; and for many a time*
> *I have been half in love with easeful Death . . .*[12]

In fact Mary Tighe used this word several times with a certain resonance that Keats would have appreciated. In the Bodleian Library in Oxford there is a very small copy of *Psyche; or, The Legend of Love* published in 1805, the first edition of fifty copies. It is bound in cream leather with fine gold tooling and there are two white pages at the beginning inscribed with sonnets, one to Mary Tighe from Barbara Wilmot, Lady Dacre, a literary friend who was also a poet, to whom the copy is dedicated, and the other to Barbara Wilmot from Mary Tighe, who writes:

---

\* temple

*Alas! For me, in anguish and in fear,*
*The darkling days have since roll'd heavily.*

Keats knew exactly what 'darkling days' were, and this perhaps bound him to Mary Tighe in ways he could hardly understand. Their vocabulary was a shared vocabulary because of their literary inheritance and because they both worked under the dark shadow of tuberculosis and early death.

*The Dying Keats by Joseph Severn*

Keats's sonnet of 1816 'On the Grasshopper and the Cricket' tells memorably of the grasshopper:

*The poetry of earth is never dead:*
*When all the birds are faint with the hot sun,*
*And hide in cooling trees, a voice will run*
*From hedge to hedge about the new-mown mead.*[13]

Mary Tighe's poem 'The Grass-Hopper', or 'Little Progeny of Spring' is written out in her meticulous hand in the 1805 'Verses transcribed for HT' (The Brompton Volumes). The poem is touching proof of the common concerns of John Keats and Mary Tighe:

*Little progeny of spring!*
*To the light-winged Zephyr born,*
*Thoughtless, idle, chirping thing,*
*Gayest tenant of the morn!*

*Cherished still by Ceres' care,*
*Dear to Phoebus ever thou!*
*Truly they have bid thee share,*
*All that yields the fruitful plough.*

*While the fragrant turf is green,*
*While the yellow harvests wave,*
*All that culture's eye hath seen,*
*All that earth profusely gave,*

*All is thine! Behold for thee*
*Their milky arms the lilies spread!*
*And the dewy nectar see*
*O'er thy drunken goblets shed!*[14]

## NOTES

1 Sonnet: 'Addressed to my Brother', 1805 published by H. Buxton Forman as John Keats's work.

2 Buxton Forman's note for this sonnet in his edition of John Keats's poetry, 1883.

3 'To Some Ladies on Receiving a Curious Shell' by John Keats.

4 'Ode to a Nightingale' by John Keats, 1819.

5 'The Eve of St Agnes', Stanza 24, by John Keats, 1819.

6 'Psyche; or, The Legend of Love', Canto 1, lines 397-405.

7 'Psyche; or, The Legend of Love', Canto 6 lines 460-77.

8 'The Eve of St Agnes', Stanza 36, by John Keats, 1819.

9 Letter to George Keats, December 1818.

10 Sonnet: 'To Spenser', by John Keats, 1818.

11 'Ode to Psyche', by John Keats, 1819.

12 'Ode to a Nightingale', by John Keats, 1819.

13 'On the Grasshopper and the Cricket', by John Keats, 1816.

14 'On the Grasshopper', by Mary Tighe, 1805, The Brompton Volumes NLI 5495.

# CHAPTER 11

# AT DOMINICK STREET
## *'The prison couch'*

Just north of the centre of Dublin lies Henrietta Street and not far to the east is Dominick Street. Both roads still contain splendid examples of domestic architecture of the eighteenth century. The town houses front the street with wide and deep flights of steps to allow an easy berth to the extravagantly wide dresses of the period and the broad doors have fanlights in the glass above, each a different pattern. Today they are massive, crumbling Georgian residences, their pitted, unpointed bricks a pockmarked testimony to the past. In her *Reminiscences*, Caroline Hamilton writes about the location of her grandfather's house in Dublin which he purchased to stay in on his journeys up to town from Woodstock: 'Sir William Fownes bought Number 37 Dominick Street [today Number 40] on account of its contiguity to Henrietta Street, where most of Lady Betty's family lived and from its being in one of the most fashionable parts of the town.'[1] The five storeys of Number 40 are sandwiched today between two Schools of English, but the house is nonetheless structurally much as it was when Mary Tighe retired there to enjoy her last days in Dublin society. To the left at the front, a great arch arises to allow carriages through to the stables at the back. The pillars round the front door diminish gently towards the top into a cluster of stone roses and scrolls. The steps are so worn that they slope towards the street, steps up which the often weary Mary climbed each day for as long as she could, until it became clear that she could not continue to walk.

The visit to Hannah More had taken place in the summer of 1804 and in December she moved to Brompton 'in the neighborhood of London' to stay in the residence of her brother John before making a trip with her mother to Pargate near Chester on the Dee and returning to Ireland in the summer of 1805. The Irish Sea crossing was discouragingly rough and Mary did not leave again after their return. She was a very sick woman and had written from London to her cousin Caroline just before she left:

> I have had severe weather and felt it severely, in spite of our six Thermometers, roaring fires and constant warmth which has been so effectively kept up in my rooms, that during this whole hard winter, I have never had my hands cold, not known anything of the frost except its influence on my chest which is unconceivable. Vaughan shakes his head and says with a disappointed air, 'Ah! she must breathe our air though we do warm it' – My nights have been, in general, much better this last month, but that is decidedly the effect of medicine, and I am obliged to change the opiates continually as each loses its effect. The first nights of a medicine are to me indeed blessed Sabbaths and my spirits are better than they have been at times when my strength and health had not 'failed me'.[2]

Mary Tighe's visits to her London physician had been successful in one sense; she had learned to accept her illness, to understand how to manage the disease as best she could with the help of opiates and nursing care. However, her brother John's failing marriage had been a source of discomfiture to herself and to her mother, as was the behaviour at this time of Harry:

> The year 1805 was a sad one. I saw my son in contact with a woman I believed to be profligate and knew to be profane, imperious and violent. I knew that Harry was treading crooked paths and witnessed the daily decline of my poor suffering child. Dreadful post of observation. Darker every hour![3]

It was troubling that John's marriage was not happy. It appears that the 'woman' mentioned above is Camilla, and Theodosia's comment that she was 'profligate' suggests that she was unfaithful to John at this time, an anticipation of the final cause of their divorce – her adultery with a mutual friend. If the woman mentioned by Theodosia is someone outside John's marriage, the implications are no less alarming. Perhaps because of anxiety about her brother's welfare, Mary did not choose to go abroad to Lisbon or Madeira, as Dr Vaughan had suggested, but travelled home with the Blachfords, who now had a son (an earlier child had died on their travels in Italy), and with William Tighe and family. To talk to William was comforting. He gave his own independent view of events in the family and recommended that Mary stay in Ireland now, near to him and his household at Woodstock. The Blachfords all stayed at Dominick Street but Theodosia writes:

> This visit was not very pleasant to either party. Indeed, no one could, I think, ever find Camilla a pleasant guest and both Mary and Henry found her a jealous and not good-natured spy and in many respects oppressive. I was very glad when she left them.[4]

The Blachfords left town and took a house at Vevai near Bray, Co. Wicklow.

That Harry was 'treading crooked paths' might have been felt as yet more troubling, and indeed it no doubt was. The remark is made by Theodosia in such close contingency to her adverse comments about John's relationship that it is difficult to see it as anything except a condemnation of Harry's meetings with other women. Yet at this time, in the Blachford's residence in Brompton, Mary started a collection of poems for Harry which she dedicated to him. She wrote out each poem by hand and decorated it with a small water-colour painting. The volume is beautifully executed and there is no doubt that it represents a kind of acceptance of their marriage which up till now had been hard to achieve. She acknowledges that she has left Harry in spirit to write her poetry, to explore her own world and that he in his turn has wandered, yet returns to her.

For whom did Mary Tighe write? To some extent, simply for family and close friends, as is exemplified by the carefully handwritten volumes for Henry Tighe executed at Brompton in 1805. At this time, her advisers encouraged her to publish, but Mary was reluctant. Did she not see herself as a fully fledged author? Were her mother's demands that she quit literature still preying on her mind? It seems most likely that she simply lacked confidence and encouragement from those very close to her. In a letter to Joseph Cooper Walker (December 1804) she wrote that she had:

> . . . myself been on the verge of a most frightful auspice and had almost been persuaded to expose to the mercy of the reviewers, Edinburgh butchers & all, my poor little Psyche & volume of smaller poems which I was advis'd to add, as I might, to save the straw-like appendages of a kite, that she might not fall to the ground by her own weight – however after a few nights agitation I found that I have not nerves for it.[5]

But in 1805 *Psyche; or, The Legend of Love* was printed in Ireland in a private edition of fifty copies which were passed around among Mary's friends and given to the Ladies of Llangollen, Thomas Moore, William Parnell, Anna Seward, Lady Dacre, Sarah Tighe and Elinor Ward, amongst many others. Perhaps Mary Tighe had achieved what she wanted to in terms of publication. Avid readers circulated their copies and transcribed the poem for friends. The Tighe family today owns a neatly written, much-thumbed exercise book which contains a full copy of 'Psyche' made by a relative. In the Bodleian Library in Oxford a very small, beautifully tooled but much read edition has a poem to Mary's friend, Mrs Barbara Wilmot, later Lady Dacre, pasted into the flyleaf (*opposite page*).

The charm and goodwill of Vaughan had given Mary extra zest. She wanted to make the most of what remained of her life and she now had sufficient confidence in herself to say what she wanted to do. The publication of her work, although only fifty copies were made, brought her celebrity on her return to Dublin. Theodosia writes that Mary said she was visited 'by troops of friends' and Caroline claims that although she was clearly very ill indeed, they all vied with each other to see who could contribute most to her amusement:

> Mary's sufferings seemed to encrease [*sic*] daily and neither the smiles of Lady Charlemont, the kind looks of William Parnell, nor the visits of Lady Asgill & Sir Arthur Wellesley, Duke of Wellington, nor the coarser flattery of Lydia Whyte, could stop the progress of her disease – in a note to me she said that many of her days were 'lost to her' from

her incapability of doing anything but sit with her head leaning on the pillowed arm of her couch in a state between sleeping and waking & during every night her sufferings from difficulty of breathing were very great and sometimes 'her head' she said 'never for one moment reposed on her pillow' yet on what she called her 'well days' her friends left her very few minutes alone after two o'clock.[6]

---

*To M:<sup></sup> Wilmot*

Lady forgive, if late the languid lyre,
    At length responsive to thy sweetest lay,
    Breathe the low, trembling strain, with weak essay
To utter all which grateful thoughts inspire :
Forgive, if, vacant of poetic fire,
    I seem with frigid heart, and dull delay,
    The flatt'ring summons careless to obey :
Woo'd, kindly woo'd so highly to aspire,
    And echo the soft name of friend ; for me,
Alas! for me, in anguish, and in fear,
    The darkling days have since roll'd heavily.
But let my Psyche in thy partial ear
    Whisper the sad excuse, & smiling see
In hers the lovely sister form most fair, most dear.

*Tighe*

---

William was among the many visitors to the sitting room at Dominick Street where the invalid lay upon her sofa. He and his brother Harry took over the leadership of the Commons group who opposed Union, voting against the motion in 1799 and again in 1800. They decided that if the sick Grattan could be persuaded to return as a member for Wicklow there was then some chance of the Act of Union being rejected. The election was allowed by the Sheriff at the last minute and on 15 January 1800, early in the morning, William and his brother Harry called to Henry Grattan's house and asked him to come with them to College Green. 'Why don't you let me die in peace?' he said in despair. But, persuaded by his wife, he went to the Commons and he said in February 1800:

> The Union then, is not an identification of the two nations; it is merely a merger of the parliament of one nation in that of the other; one nation, namely England, retains her full proportion; Ireland strikes off two-thirds; she does so, without any regard either to her present number or to comparative physical strength; she is more than one third in population, in territory, and less than one sixth in representation. Thus there is no identification in anything, save only in legislature, in which there is complete and absolute absorption. It follows that the two nations are not identified, though the Irish legislature be absorbed, and, by that act of absorption, the feeling of one of the nations is not identified but alienated.[7]

But the Act of Union was passed and the Irish Houses of Parliament were closed. At Dominick Street they all lamented the demise of Grattan's Parliament. The Irish Parliament had been abolished but The Castle government remained in place and England and Ireland were to be regarded as a single economic unit. Those representing Irish constituencies were now expected to journey to Westminster when the House was sitting and there were to be only one hundred Irish representatives, a reduction in numbers which meant that some boroughs were cut back, eighty were disenfranchised and compensation paid to the incumbent MP, and others were grouped together to be represented by one. William Tighe was paid compensation but there was a sense of disappointment and frustration which could not be ignored. Matters such as the all-important one of

Catholic Emancipation were set aside, yet Catholic demands were as strong as ever – they subsided underground and would emerge later all the stronger for their secret life. William consistently honoured his pledges made before the Act of Union and stuck to his commitment to the reform of the tithe system in Ireland, which, as a landlord, he knew to be corrupt in many parts of the country. He voted for Catholic relief at every opportunity and opposed the salary increase for the Irish Viceroy; he had seen years of lavish splendour at the Castle and knew it was time such excess was brought to an end. He wrote to his mother: 'I shall never swerve from one principle, both as religious and political, namely that, a religious difference ought never to make a civil disqualification.'[8]

All these matters required much discussion in the Tighe manner and Mary liked to join in whenever she could, lying on her couch in the drawing room and giving her view. Armed with her range of opiate-based drugs, she could at least manage her own pain relief as she moved towards the later stages of tuberculosis, and shape for herself moments of calm within each day when friends could be summoned to read with her, to talk, or simply to join in a conversational group to which she was a quiet listener:

> After 1805, Mrs Tighe chiefly resided in Dominick Street, Dublin, and was so far enfeebled by constant illness that she lost the use of her limbs, and was obliged to lie always on the sofa. Notwithstanding this affliction, her vigour of mind was unimpaired and she received constant assemblies of all that was most intellectual in Dublin society. Around that lovely and patient invalid's couch might be seen gathered Lady Charlemont, Lady St George, Lydia Whyte, vain Sydney Owenson, with her carefully arranged scarf, and Thomas Moore.[9]

There were three visitors apart from William whom Mary found particularly interesting at this time and they were Arthur Wellesley, Thomas Moore and Sydney Owenson. Arthur Wellesley, later to be the Duke of Wellington, brought news of what was happening in the city. But as well as this, he could talk of the old days at the Castle, the days when he had first met and loved Kitty Pakenham, the woman he was to marry. And Thomas Moore, the Irish poet, was one with whom the subject of relationships

*Sydney Owenson, Lady Morgan by René Théodore Berthon*

could be broached. He was all for love and all for poetry. He teased and cajoled Mary with his quips and wit and read his poems to her as soon as he had written them. He knew she liked to be thought of as a literary person and wrote in a letter in 1806: 'One hardly used to get a peep at her bluestockings, but now I am afraid, she shows them up to the knee.'

The novelist, Sydney Owenson, later to be Lady Morgan, was known for her eccentric dress-sense in an age when very few women would go out to a formal occasion at the Castle or dine out without a 'high' wig and full court dress. But the small, youthful Owenson wore a simple white muslin frock like a girl. Mary's style of dress was unfashionably simple too. But Sydney Owenson had an enviable social confidence, a vigour and outspokenness that were the very opposite of Mary's modest manner and she was fascinated and repelled by such open assertiveness and secretly longed for such assurance herself. They were rivals, though neither could admit it. Owenson's first real success came in 1806 with the publication of *The Wild Irish Girl*, a novel about Ireland in which she broached political issues. The daughter of a travelling Irish actor and his Protestant wife Jane Hill, she was born in 1770 and became a support to her father if not the breadwinner of the family after her mother died in 1789. Her path often crossed with that of Mary Tighe. Owenson published ten novels in her lifetime and was in a strong position to advise her on finishing her novel *Selena*.

Sometimes Arthur Wellesley told Mary about the history of his family. The Wellesleys had lived longer than the Tighes in Ireland. The earliest document in which their name appears is a charter dated about 1180 in the archives of Wells Cathedral and there is documentary evidence of a Wellesley in Ireland by the reign of Henry III. From the latter half of the fourteenth century onwards, they lived entirely in Ireland, steadily amassing land by marriage or services rendered. Ever since they settled, they had been intermarrying within that restricted circle of the Anglo-Norman families of the Pale among whom they lived: the Plunkets of Dunsany, the Fitzgeralds of Dangan and Kildare, the Cusacks of Dangan and Trim, the Colleys of Castle Carbery, who were his ancestors. The number of families was small, which accounts for cousins marrying cousins, thereby keeping the power and wealth within the select band. There is no doubt but that the Wellesley boys – Arthur had four brothers – grew up with a strong sense of belonging to the ruling class, despite a sometimes embarrassing lack of funds to support that sense of destiny.

Arthur shared an Irish childhood with Mary and Henry Tighe, though not a privileged one. Changes of school, the death of his father in 1781, and the sense of being 'only' the third son made for a troubled, unconfident adolescence. A musical boy, he had inherited his father's ability to play the violin but once he entered formal education, there was little opportunity to develop this skill. He was sent to Eton as his father had planned but he stayed for three years and left. Arthur was never an academic star and he found it difficult to settle into a large group of boys, amongst whom he had no especial talent. Richard, the eldest brother and now head of the family, advised that Arthur should leave Eton so that funds could be concentrated on the younger boys. His progress was constantly updated in letters to Sarah Tighe from the Ladies of Llangollen, who lived near Arthur's maternal grandmother, Lady Dungannon. Sarah Ponsonby wrote to Sarah Tighe that Arthur was 'backward'. Next came a successful spell at a riding school at Angers in France which seems to have turned the tables for the young Wellesley, who then got a commission in the Army and returned to his mother, Lady Mornington, who suddenly found she had a swan for a son after all. He emerged as an accomplished horseman and spoke good French. He could now be sent out into the world.

As Mary lay on her couch in the sitting room at Dominick Street, she would reminisce with Arthur Wellesley about their visits to see the Ladies of Llangollen and Mary would admit to him that their rural but independent way of life was what she would have liked for herself. He had visited Llangollen in the summer of 1784 with his sister Anne and his 'polished' brother, Gerald. Lady Eleanor noted Arthur as 'A charming young man, handsome, fashioned, tall and elegant'. It was at this point in his so far not very illustrious career that Wellesley engaged with the question of what he wanted to do, and his eldest brother acquired a commission for him into the Army as an aide-de-camp to the Lord Lieutenant in Dublin. Arthur happily packed up and went back to the land of his childhood. It was February 1788, and Mary Tighe had already made her debut at the Castle. As aide-de-camp, many of Arthur's duties were to help organise the social life of the court of the Viceroy and the two met at this point. And he met and wooed his future wife, Kitty Pakenham, at the Castle balls. But her father, Lord Longford, discouraged his bright daughter from becoming engaged to the man with whom she had fallen in love. Lord Longford was determined his daughter should marry well and Arthur was forced to beat a retreat, though very reluctantly. He burnt his violin, symbol of his sensitive nature and vowed that he would find a way to return to claim Kitty. With a commission as Major, he set off for his first real battle experience in Flanders and resolved to study tactics himself.

Arthur Wellesley's regiment was sent to India, by which time he was Colonel and these years were the making of Wellesley. His strength as soldier and tactician became clear and when he returned home in 1805, he was a wealthy man with acknowledged prowess as a military leader. Napoleon had been proclaimed Emperor in May 1804. Arthur had not communicated with Kitty Pakenham during their time apart, but each had waited for the other since the time when he had proposed to her in 1793, the year that France declared war on Britain, and he was rejected as unsuitable. The faithful pair reopened their courtship after thirteen years. Mary was moved as she listened to the soldier and recognised him as an entirely different man from the one at the Castle who had danced so closely with Kitty. He had kept his word as a man of honour – he was true to his youthful promise to love her, but was it right for them to continue their relationship? What if they found, as had she and Harry, that early passion could soon wear thin? Her doubts were not unfounded. On 10 April 1806 Kitty Pakenham married Arthur Wellesley, and Mary's death in 1810 prevented her from knowing the later sad story of Kitty's imperfect relationship with her renowned husband, her loneliness and sense of inadequacy in the shadow of her husband's worldly success.

Wellesley had stood as MP for Trim, Co. Meath. The Tighe brothers and Wellesley would often sit and talk of these new times of the Union, of how Ireland had prospered in the time of Grattan's parliament. But what drew Mary Tighe to this now attractively confident young man was his experience as a soldier, his knowledge of India and its people, his determination to succeed. Something in Mary's character chimed with Wellesley: her willingness to pit herself against the odds when they were stacked against her; her love of writing and the amount of writing she had done despite her illness, and her struggle in adversity gave her character a strength to which he

*Thomas Moore*
*after Sir Thomas Lawrence*

responded. And perhaps the violinist in him, shut down so long ago, awakened in the room in Dominick Street where Tom Moore sometimes sang his ballads and Mary read her poems in her quiet but precise voice, speaking of another world of the heart and the mind conjoined, which Wellesley knew to be slipping out of his reach. In the summer of 1808, when Kitty's second son was born, Wellesley left Cork to join the forces fighting against Napoleon in the Iberian Peninsula. When he returned to Ireland, Mary Tighe was dead.

Thomas Moore was Mary's Irish contemporary and was thought of as Ireland's special national poet; as Burns belonged to the Scots, so Tom Moore was Ireland's minstrel. His poems and ballads were set to music, and many are still remembered. His biographies of Sheridan, of Lord Edward Fitzgerald and of Byron, who was a close and demanding friend, are mentioned in the bibliographies of other better-known works. Like Mary Tighe, he was acclaimed in his day and he is remembered by poems such as: 'The Minstrel Boy', 'The Last Rose of Summer', 'The Harp that once through Tara's Hall', 'The meeting of the waters' and 'Oft in the stilly night'.

Mary Tighe became a close and dear friend. Moore visited her often in the Dublin years leading up to her death, arriving at the house in Dominick Street for literary discussions at 'little evening parties' with the young poet who knew well that there were not many such moments left to her. The sound of his footstep at the door always cheered her as he burst into the house and called her name. Tom Moore's natural good humour and his love of social life made him a welcome companion at any party. He would tell tales about the rich and famous, read aloud or sing and bring his latest verses to share with Mary's visitors.

She was latterly confined not only to the house but to her couch, yet the early part of each day was still spent in Study and she had often little evening parties where Moore sang his sweetest songs to a few (perhaps not more than eight or ten) of those who were then most esteemed in Dublin, for rank or talents. Moore visited her constantly and often submitted his works for her criticism while they were yet in manuscript. He showed her one little poem and by her countenance, which was capable of the greatest expression, he saw that she highly disapproved of it – he threw it into the fire – but some months afterwards it appeared in print.[10]

Especially significant is the poem published in 1803: 'To Mrs Henry Tighe, on reading her "Psyche"':

> *One maid there was who round her lyre*
> *The mystic myrtle wildly wreath'd;-*
> *But all her sighs were sighs of fire*
> *The myrtle wither'd as she breath'd.*[11]

This is a fine tribute and a tender one. Moore was twenty-six and his only rival to fame as Ireland's poet was Mary herself. He himself had sometimes been accused of abandoning the problems of his native land and of running away to London to meet the celebrated men and women of the day. Here in Dublin the two poets compared their work, they discussed the state of the nation and everyone present would join in to keep the conversation going if the patient flagged and her head fell onto her pillow. Sometimes she would think of her own timidity as a young girl, of how she had felt she must hide her intelligence. Yet after the publication of *Psyche; or The Legend of Love* she was, Caroline Hamilton says, 'visited by those who were then most esteemed in Dublin for rank and talent'.[12]

In October 1806 Mary developed rheumatic fever with violent symptoms that threatened to destroy her. After this illness, it seemed she would not walk again, 'her limbs were gone for ever'. But by the summer of the following year she suddenly rallied and it became possible to plan a series of farewell visits in her carriage to places she had loved. She went to Altidore Castle, the house in which her father, William Blachford, was born and where her brother, John now lived with his son, Camilla having left to spend time abroad. Rossana was visited, as was Westaston, the seat of Thomas Acton. They stayed for a while with her cousin Caroline and Charles Hamilton at Hamwood House, Dunboyne, Co. Meath, with the La Touche family at Mullacash, Co. Kildare, and with the family of Sir John and Lady Power at Kilfane House, Thomastown, Co. Kilkenny. And of course they visited Woodstock, the home of William Tighe and his wife Marianne, where Mary was to return later because it suited her best of all. In June 1808 she wrote a sonnet for William Parnell, younger son of Sir John Parnell and grandfather of Charles Stewart Parnell, on the occasion of her last visit to Avondale House which was set in fine grounds on the way to Rossana.

The poem of March 1808 'To Lady Charlemont, in Return for her Presents of Flowers', makes a public declaration of Mary's gratitude to those 'troops of friends' who have visited her, and does so with ingenuity and grace:

> *For, as thy hand with smiling flowers*
> *Hath crowned the lingering, wintry hours,*
> *Even thus for me affection's care*
> *Hath sheltered from the nipping air*
> *The tender buds of half-chilled hope*
> *That seemed in withering gloom to droop,*
> *And bid them bloom, revived again,*
> *In spite of years and grief and pain.*
> *O'er me Affection loves to spread*
> *Her comforts full, unmeasured;*
> *To bless my smiling hearth she sends*
> *The dearer smile of dearest friends,*
> *And bids my prison couch assume*
> *No form of pain, no air of gloom;*
> *But sweet content and cheerful ease,*
> *All that in solitude can please,*
> *And all that soothing, social love*
> *Can bid its quiet favourites prove,*
> *Wooed by the voice of tenderness,*
> *Unite my happy home to bless.*[13]

The 'prison couch' has been transformed into a soothing, painless place and her flagging spirits have been revived like spring buds or tender flowers because of the warmth of friends' thoughtfulness on her behalf. Her life has taken shape again despite several journeys to the edge. Thus the sad years of depression and illness in the grips of consumption are re-evaluated. Mary has found a new way of living and of writing; she has discovered herself to be part of a small orchestra, a group of friends. The days of solitary practice playing the harp to release her grief are nearly over.

NOTES

1 Caroline Hamilton: *Reminiscences*, NLI 4810.
2 Caroline Hamilton: *Mary Tighe*, NLI 4810.
3 Theodosia Blachford: *Observations on the Journal of Mary Tighe*, NLI 4810.
4 ibid.
5 Letter from Mary Tighe to Joseph Walker, December 1804.
6 Caroline Hamilton: *Mary Tighe*, NLI 4810.
7 Grattan's speech to The Commons, February, 1800.
8 William Tighe to Sarah Tighe, 17 June 1811, PRONI.
9 Caroline Hamilton: *Mary Tighe*, NLI 4810.
10 ibid.
11 Thomas Moore: 'To Mrs Henry Tighe, On Reading her "Psyche"'.
12 Caroline Hamilton: *Mary Tighe*, NLI 4810.
13 'To Lady Charlemont: in Return for her Presents of Flowers', March 1808.

# CHAPTER 12

# WILLIAM 'STATISTICAL' TIGHE

## *A 'mind strong by nature'*

A welcome visitor who came to sit in the chair beside Mary's couch in the drawing room at Dominick Street was William Tighe. They discussed what was happening in the aftermath of the Rebellion in Ireland, read poetry together, or perhaps listened to Tom Moore recite, if it was a day when he was there. William gave everyone news of his family at Inistioge. He did not reappear as a significant part of Mary's life until her consumption was confirmed, her peregrination around the spas of England in search of some kind of cure was at an end. Sometimes when they were on their own, they talked over the past, of how he had left for the Grand Tour at the time when young Harry had unswervingly moved in to start to woo her on returning from boarding school. Mary told him of the mutual agreement that she and Harry now had – to enjoy their lives as best they could for the present.

William's Grand Tour took him in January 1788 to Paris, Orléans and again in August to Paris, where he was joined by his mother and younger

*William Tighe of Rossana*
*(1766-1816)*

siblings; they then all travelled together to the Lowlands. Mary laughed at Sarah's decision not to go as far as Italy for fear her hair might turn white with anxiety. The family went home in October 1788 and William went on to Rome, where Pompeo Batoni had painted his father's portrait in 1763 when he was on the Grand Tour. Batoni was the most popular artist of all and was chosen by many young English and Irish men of the period as well as by young Romans who gathered in his studios to socialise and meet visitors. He was highly accomplished and managed to convey a sense of social standing and ease in his subjects, who always appear to have brought with them a copious and extravagant wardrobe. The details and language of dress are beautifully displayed and are part of the means by which the painter conveys the character of his sitter.

It was in 1788, Mary told William, that she first developed what her mother described as a 'most extraordinary cough, a spasm, every day from two to nine in the evening', probably the first evidence of the onset of tuberculosis. He told her of his return to Paris in 1789 and of all he had seen of the Revolution, of his divided loyalties and how he knew that one day there would be rebellion in Ireland. He decided to extend his tour

and over the next two years he travelled on to Vienna and Budapest, Warsaw, St Petersburg and Stockholm. In January 1791 he was off to Berlin, in June to Dresden, and July to Switzerland where Mary's brother John Blachford met him. When he returned in 1792 he had been away four years.

William was now ready to settle at home. The Grand Tour was a happy educative 'year out' for the sons of the wealthy in the eighteenth century and young men travelled through Europe, often staying for a period in Rome, a fine centre for improving their classical

*William Tighe senior, painted by Pompeo Batoni in Rome in 1763*

and Renaissance education. Many used it as an opportunity to grace great houses at home with works of art bought abroad, which became emblems of their cultivated life. Most used the tour as an experience in growing up, taking the freedom as a means to find their way in society and to gain experience of life. At home at Rossana, Sarah Tighe feared for her own son William when she heard drifts of gossip. 'Italy is particularly dangerous to young men' she said. But despite his mother's trepidations, William flourished.

As she listened to the tales of William's Grand Tour, Mary reminded herself that he was fatherless, just as Sarah was husbandless. In her letters Sarah asked persistently about the family estate and financial matters, wondering if and when they could rebuild the local church at Inistioge, what she could do to alleviate her deteriorating financial situation and reminding her eldest born of his duties. 'Billy', as Sarah called him, had drawn money on his Dublin account and his mother had spotted the transaction:

> By your draft from Paris we have reason to think that you are there and are much concerned that you have grown so neglectful of your friends. We have not heard from you these three months. We all wish we could persuade you to come home, satisfied that you would appear in a more respectable light and be infinitely more happy than rambling about. There are a thousand reasons why you ought to return at this time, but that which will perhaps have the most weight is what your friend Mr Lloyd suggested when I saw him last – the expected dissolution of parliament when it will be necessary for you to appoint proper Members to represent your Boroughs. If you are so near, it would be well if you spend at least this summer at home, to regulate the affairs of a family of which you are now the head and who all look up to you for advice and protection…it seems your duty to come back to Woodstock, which I hope you consider as your own. Having given it to you, it is awkward to give orders, and I have constant applications for them.[1]

William's strongest card, as young travellers have discovered over the ages, was not to reply at all to his mother's irritating and distressing fits of anxiety about him. But sometimes he fired off an angry riposte. On 6 October 1790 he wrote from Stockholm:

It was not till today that I received your letter of the 29th of August. Tho' I have been here a fortnight – I am sorry you should have any apprehensions on my account – but to write at a regular or fixed time is what I do not think I should be able to do were I to be fixed in one place – but to write a letter once a week would be somewhat curious when eight days or seven nights in a carriage without entering an Inn – or would you have had me copy the log book or written a sea journal when I was lying in a couch tossing in the midst of the Baltic – in what sailors call 'a fresh gale'?[2]

William tried to establish his right not to reply but he remained intensely involved with Ireland, as the angry words of the following letter convey. He alludes to the sale of peerages and the reputation of Irish peers for drunkenness. As MP for Banagher from 1789 he was reprimanded for his absence from the Irish parliament and on 18 March 1791 he wrote from Berlin:

Kings have long arms, but I never knew before that a sergeant-at-arms was so gifted by his office. He may stretch and stretch till he bursts like an ambitious frog before I shall ever be able to see the point of his middle finger approaching Berlin. None but an Irish parliament could take a man into custody at a thousand miles distance and keep a man in custody who was wandering where he pleased. I am one of thirteen members who never attend the Irish House; but if the 287 (including their noble speaker) can do such little good, a dozen doubtful votes will be but a feather in the scale against the decided weight of corruption. Before they restrained the sale of whiskey they should have restrained the sale of peerages. Was [*sic*] you to hire a house, would you not sweep the parlour before you washed out the pig-sty?

I occupy the same apartment that Mirabeau did in 1786 – I am writing perhaps in the spot that he did – and he could not but have felt behind him a spirit in the air of the room sufficient to turn the head of his weaker successors.[3]

William's reference to Mirabeau suggests his Republican sympathies, as does his impatience with the abuse of power of landlords and MPs in his native country. His anger is healthy and when he returned he became a fully fledged member of his family who engaged with integrity in the problems of his country and was seldom absent from home, except as an Irish MP at Westminster after the Act of Union in 1801.

Much as Sarah resented her son's long absence and all the domestic burdens imposed upon her by the management of the estates of Rossana and Woodstock, she was forced to recognise on his return the welcome growth in maturity that his travels had conferred upon him. He chose his wife carefully. Letters from Mary in Dublin to William's sister Bess Tighe about his marriage to Marianne suggest a young woman's enthusiasm for a wedding and at that stage at least no sense of rivalry with the girl who had been chosen at last by William. 'Billy's approaching marriage has had to be postponed because of Miss Gahan's chickenpox which she has had very violently, much worse than any of us were the time we had it at Rossana…but I hope she may not be as long mark'd by it as I was – her face has now a great deal – one eye almost closed and she has kept her bed for six days – I do not know how Billy bears the necessary absence. People say they suppose he is in a terrible way! But I have not seen him this some time, so I cannot judge.'[4]

Life at Woodstock proceeded harmoniously over a number of years when William and Marianne Tighe first lived there as a newly married couple and started to raise their family. The other 'M. Tighe' – Marianne – had a son first, whom she named William, and her letters of 1795 reflect her love, indeed adoration of her young husband. When he was away for a few days or busy in Dublin with parliamentary sessions, she wrote affectionate notes, which form a bright contrast to the sad, darker relationship of Harry and Mary:

> I am waiting in anxious expectation for the arrival of the Post, in the hopes of getting a letter from my dearest love. I long so much to know when I shall see you again…I want you to comfort me dearest William. I am not happy without you. You are the only person to whom I would tell anything that was the matter with me. Perhaps you will say that trying a person with complaints is an odd proof of love…Dearest dearest William Believe me yours ever, M. Tighe.[5]

The very next day she writes again and ends thus: 'Little William is very well – I am getting a go-cart for him to teach him to walk. Adieu my best love and greatest comfort.' Indeed these letters – signed M. Tighe, as above – may have been responsible for later generations significantly confusing Mary Tighe and Marianne Tighe.

William and his wife Marianne successfully extended the gardens and the buildings of Woodstock and lived there in great style and comfort with their three children, William, Daniel and Hannah. Marianne Gahan was the only child of a wealthy man, Daniel Gahan, and his wife Hannah Bunbury of Coolquil, Co.Tipperary. After the death of her maternal uncle, Marianne received a considerable inheritance which went to William. The chickenpox was the worst of their early problems and although their marriage has the air of a strategically planned arrangement, they settled down well and soon became fond of one another. William, or Billy as the family liked to call him, had grown up at Woodstock with his mother's parents and he felt a strong sense of identity with the house and surrounding lands: this was his home. After his grandfather Sir William Fownes died in 1778 there was no resident landlord. Since his return from the Grand Tour, William had been working with tenants and estate workers to rejuvenate the estate. The approach to the house was to be changed: a new drive a mile long was dug and laid by local workers and a very grand pair of plinths was erected to support the gates, each topped with a sculpted wolf.

*The gates at Woodstock*

On the approach to the house, the land dropped away to the River Nore and there were deer in the park on the right. With seeds gathered on his travels abroad, William created orchards and gardens and planted exotic trees on the lawns. A coach house went up and a chalet for picnics and parties, called Swiss Cottage, was built at a suitable distance in the woods; in true Romantic style, it stood on a craggy summit of rock looking down the glen to the sound of a waterfall which fell a little above the cottage, providing a proper sense of the 'sublime'. Grandfather Fownes had built the Red House on the River Nore and William refurbished it for entertaining guests and cruising on the water. William loved Woodstock because it was where he spent his childhood and because of its association with Sir William Fownes, and also as a place from which as a botanist he could collect plants and observe them in their natural habitat throughout the year. All these improvements were made before 1800. After 1800 two wings were added on either side of the main house, turning a plain mansion into a Palladian residence, as was the fashion of the day. William was much influenced by his time in Italy and it was this that gave him the inspiration. The living space was vastly increased and the elegant extensions nicely matched the main house in style and finish. The coach house and stable block were rebuilt to grander proportions so that a proper number of visitors could be received.

*Woodstock with the extensions added by William Tighe in the early 1800s*

William Tighe liked to think of himself as a member of a group of gentlemen-scientists of the period and a poet as well. In 1808 he published 'The Plants, A Poem with Notes and Occasional Poems by William Tighe Esq, London 1808'. At the start of the second volume of the British Library copy in William's hand is written:

*To The Rt Hon Sir Joseph Banks, Bart*
*With the author's best compliments, May 18ᵗʰ [1811]*

'The Plants' is signed on the first page *Jos. Banks*. As president of the Royal Society, Joseph Banks liked to keep in touch with what was happening in the world of science from his house in Soho. He received visitors such as William Tighe, who saw himself as a botanist and had in 1802 had published *Maritime plants observed on the coast of the County of Wexford*.

John Blachford also considered himself a member of the scientific set, conversing with William about farming, for he had recently moved back to Altidore Castle, the family home where he had lived as a boy after his

*A newly erected replica of the conservatory at Woodstock*

father's death. Here he settled happily to become a noted agriculturalist of his day, as well as a skilled chemist, addressing the problems of the estate and in 1812 Thomas Radcliffe reported on the 'extensive and luxuriant crops of turnip, corn and meadow'. Mary's pleasure was heartfelt when she went to visit him in 1807 on her last tour: to find her brother happily installed on the family estate, to see his young son enjoying the countryside she had known as child, was to her a special fulfilment. She was not to know of his later happiness when in 1814 he wedded Henry Grattan's daughter, Mary Ann, at Powerscourt, Co. Wicklow in a second marriage. His divorce from Camilla was by then safely over after a private Act of Parliament and scandalous revelations: John had found her in bed with William La Touche, and Henry Tighe was called as a witness in the legal proceedings.

It was as the author of *The Statistical Survey of the County of Kilkenny* that William Tighe would most like to have been remembered, and this is in fact how he is best known in Ireland where he is sometimes referred to as William *Statistical* Tighe. When Mary lay fitfully resting, recovering from her heavy dose of opium to relieve her pain, she would ask him to tell her about the estates at Woodstock and Rossana and quietly he would speak of his tenants, of their farms, their progress, their families, the birth of children, the death of the elderly. He knew every cultivated strip on each estate and, as she listened, Mary felt afresh the connection with her native land.

The population, which had probably been under two-and-a-half million in the middle of the eighteenth century, leapt to four and a half million, or perhaps more, by the end of the century. Irish agricultural practices were affected by the remoteness of many parts of the country, the lack of good communications and general lack of innovation. Only those who lived in coastal areas traded in cash, while those living in central rural areas lived in a simple subsistence economy. High rents led to arrears, arrears led to eviction. In 1799 The Royal Dublin Society petitioned Parliament for a sum to allow a Statistical Survey to be carried out. The sum was granted and in 1801 the RDS found a contributor to carry out the survey in each of the Irish counties. Two have been singled out over the years as the best: the first, Mr Weld's for County Roscommon, and the other Mr Tighe's for Kilkenny. The sum of £80 paid to each surveyor cannot possibly have rewarded the writer appropriately, for William's document is a closely written piece compiled from many thousands of statistics about local farming methods ranging from figures on the production of crops giving a total sum for arable, to a study of natural meadow, pasture and waste land, plantations, and finally, bog. The names of the parishes run down the columns like a litany of rural Ireland: Inistioge, Knocktopher, Aghaviller, Derrynahinch, Kilmagany, Dunamagin, Listerlin, Callan, Coulaghmore, Tullaroan, Killaloe, Ballycallen, Tullamaine, Fartagh, Powerstown, Grange-Sylvia, Kilmacahill, Kilbeacon, Killaghy, Rosinan, Kilcoan and Kilbride. The acreage of wheat, oats, barley, potatoes, turnips, flax is given for each. More challenging perhaps are chapters such as 'The State of the Lower Orders', or 'The State of the Poor in Kilkenny':

> The condition of the labouring poor here appears to me, from the observations I have had an opportunity of making, to be wretched in the extreme. Average hire of a day labourer is about 10d as plenty of hands can be procured at that wages, on agreeing to give them constant employment; it amounts to per year £13 without making any allowance for idle days through sickness, &c.; to which is to be added, the casual produce of the family's labour, which is supposed to amount to more than the hire of two women, or £13; but this is rather overrated, as in most cases it produces less, in many nothing: from this fund the labourer has to provide his family, which we suppose, including himself, to consist of five, as it is the average number in this neighbourhood, with food, cloathing [*sic*] firing and house rent.
>
> Consumption per day of potatoes in a family of five,
> 3 stone at 2½d or 7½ per day, per year . . . . . . . . . . . . . . .£11.13.2½
> Six quarts of sour milk, at 1d each, per annum . . . . . . . . .£9.2.6
> One ton of coals for fuel . . . . . . . . . . . . . . . . . . . . . . . . . .£1.10.0
> Rent of a cabbin per annum . . . . . . . . . . . . . . . . . . . . . . .£1.14.1½
> Cloathing . . . . . . . . . . . . . . . . . . . . . . . . . . . . . . . . . . . . .£1.10
> Total . . . . . . . . . . . . . . . . . . . . . . . . . . . . . . . . . . . . . . . .£25.9.10
> Cash for labour . . . . . . . . . . . . . . . . . . . . . . . . . . . . . . . .£26.00
> Remains to provide for sundry necessaries not
> mentioned, a balance of . . . . . . . . . . . . . . . . . . . . . . . . . .£0.10.2

The pathetically small amounts thus accounted for tell all – such sums will scarcely submit to the accounting procedures applied to them. The dependence on the potato is already a problem and the frugal amount of milk included makes it a wonder that children managed to grow at all. The Survey goes on to term the poor 'scantily supplied with potatoes, cloathed with rags, and famished with cold in their comfortless habitations'.

It is this problem that William 'Statistical' Tighe knew he had to try to resolve, not only by being an honest landlord who was always there, but also in his activities as a Member of Parliament at College Green in Dublin up to 1800, and afterwards, to the end of his life at Westminster as far as his declining health would allow. He was handicapped by the hereditary asthma which passed down the male line of the Tighe family and which caused him to have lengthy periods of illness. Time became more precious and he regarded his cousin Mary's illness with compassion. During this period she found with William the kind of intellectual companionship she had so much enjoyed with Dr Vaughan in London. They could talk over a wide range of subjects and she enjoyed reading what he had written, be it his poems, his parliamentary work, or the survey of the Kilkenny estates. He was deeply troubled by the vast inadequacies of the lives of his tenants, a problem which he knew to be at the very root of the unrest in his country. For her part, Mary considered with admiration all William's achievements and came to understand that his concerns were hers. She was not alone in her praise. In an obituary, *The Kilkenny Moderator* of 30 March 1816 spoke of him as one whose 'mind, strong by nature, was highly cultivated by erudition and enlightened by profound reflection'.

> . . . by the exercise of his genius and the practice of patriotism – by studying the felicity of his tenantry and the improvement of his neighbourhood – by promoting social intercourse and dispensing impartial justice – has embalmed his memory in his country's love, and entailed its gratitude as a freehold of his family.[6]

The life of William Tighe was a life fully lived, one of daring enterprises, of education, of patient study of various kinds, of loving and giving both to family, friends and to the community in which he lived.

And there was room to help a woman who had an incurable disease and whom he had loved briefly as a young man. It was he who would provide Mary with a safe place to die.

NOTES

1 Letter from Sarah Tighe to her son William Tighe, 8 February 1790 PRONI.

2 William Tighe to his mother, Sarah Tighe, 6 October 1790 PRONI.

3 William Tighe to his mother, Sarah Tighe, 18 March 1791 PRONI.

4 Letter from Mary Tighe to Bess Tighe, 8 May 1792 PRONI.

5 Letter from Marianne Tighe to her husband, William Tighe, 1795: MS Tighe (Woodstock) NLI 3889.

6 *The Kilkenny Moderator*, 30 March 1816.

# CHAPTER 13

# LAST VISITS
## *'Secret grief'*

She had seen her last month of May. Mary Tighe made her final journey to Rossana on 13 May 1809 from city buildings which threw their dark shadow over her failing spirit. Life in Dublin now seemed a deprivation, rather than the inspiration it had been not many years ago. Even the company of friends who had rallied to her side was tiring to her. In a letter to Caroline Hamilton she speaks of 'the black walls of Dominick Street'. The lovely grounds of Rossana with its chestnut trees, the sparkling Vartry and spacious lawns were there to be contemplated but seldom wandered in, for she could not walk any more. The 'full bloom of fragrance and beauty in the gardens' soothed her spirit. She returned to town on 8 June and set out on 13 June for Woodstock.

Mary experienced no certainty of faith of the kind she – and her mother hoped for:

> She read, I remember, about this time, a little tract, one of the first published, giving an account of a man at Bath, who was sentenced to be executed but whose fears of death were entirely removed before he left his prison by faith in Christ. 'Oh,' she said, 'how willingly would I change places with him.'[1]

The physicians decided that a change of air would be of benefit – perhaps this was the only remaining prescription they could give, and in the summer of 1809 she went to Woodstock where her mother 'had the satisfaction of seeing her removed from the flattering society which she considered so injurious to her'. Caroline assures us that 'the vigour of her mind continued unimpaired'.

In mid-June 1809 she arrived in County Kilkenny at the country seat of her cousin William, his wife Marianne and their three children. The two boys, William and Daniel, were fifteen and fourteen and they were now at Eton. Hannah, who was twelve years old, was educated by her Scottish governess. Since the Act of Union, Irish MPs attended parliament at Westminster, so William and family lived for the main part of the year in London.

At Woodstock there was more than enough room for extra family

*Mary's harp made by Sebastian Erard about 1787*

members. And there was the possibility of a picnic in the extensive grounds of the estate, a visit to the Swiss Cottage or an outing to see the walled garden take shape nearer to the house, should Mary feel well enough. A full complement of gardeners planted flowers and vegetables that summer and Woodstock looked especially beautiful to her eyes. William had taken Marianne to Italy, sometimes for a few months at a stretch and the paintings and sculptures they had acquired were placed in the new spaces of the extensions on either wing of the house. In fact, Woodstock had undergone a small renaissance as William sought to extend the house in the original spirit of the founders.

Why did she move? Was it a longing for the natural world, a desire to return to the loveliness of rural Ireland? She could have found that at Rossana, which she would have regarded as her country home, especially perhaps at Rossana Cottage built by Harry for the two of them in the years just after their marriage but, instead, she went to Woodstock to make that house her last home. This was disappointing for Harry. His

*The Nore at Inistioge seen from the path leading down from Woodstock*

elder brother had once again shown the power of his hand. But Mary felt the generosity and kindness of William; his life was rich and interesting and she fell in beside him and his family as if she were taking part in a homecoming – and quite without remorse for the years in which she had been deprived of his company. His duties at Westminster curtailed their opportunities for contact, but Mary read his long poem 'The Plants' and he made notes about her long (five-volume) novel, *Selena*, no small task, for the manuscript runs to 2,481 pages.

One of Mary's most poignant poems, 'Address to My Harp' was written about 1805 and published in 1811 in *Psyche, with Other Poems*. This instrument was a treasured possession and travelled with her whenever possible because it had been made specially for her by Sebastian Erard, who had first established himself in Paris in 1768 as a piano and harp maker and opened a branch in London in 1786 at 18 Great Marlborough Street and another later (after the French Revolution, when he left Paris) in Regent Street. His name and his first London address are inscribed on Mary's harp. Now in 1809 as her illness monopolised what remained of her life, the instrument seemed like a travelling companion, one that had seen much of her 'secret grief', of which she writes:

> *Oh, my beloved Harp! Companion dear!*
> *Sweet soother of my secret grief,*
> *No more thy sounds my soul must cheer,*
> *No more afford a soft relief.*

*When anxious cares my heart oppressed,*
*When doubts distracting tore my soul,*
*The pains which heaved my swelling breast*
*Thy gentle sway could oft control.*

*Each well remembered, practised strain,*
*The cheerful dance, the tender song,*
*Recalled with pensive, pleasing pain,*
*Some image loved and cherished long.*

*Where joy sat smiling o'er my fate,*
*And marked each bright and happy day,*
*When partial friends around me sat,*
*And taught my lips the simple lay;*

*And when by disappointment grieved*
*I saw some darling hope o'er thrown,*
*Thou hast my secret pain relieved;*
*O'er thee I wept, unseen, alone.*

*Oh! must I leave thee, must we part*
*Dear partner of my happiest days?*
*I may forget thy much-loved art,*
*Unused thy melody to raise.*[2]

This poem takes up the question of putting aside the harp, of putting aside the means by which the poet has expressed herself not only in her music-making but also in her creative writing: she senses that this too will soon cease. What was the nature of Mary Tighe's secret grief? It was in part a regression to childhood sadness, sadness at the death of the father she never knew. It was the resignation she felt when she realised quite early in life that she had consumption and was going to die young, and it was also grief at the failure of her marriage, at having borne her husband no children, at having moved, for the main part of her married life, from pillar to post without settling to make a home with him, despite having the opportunity to do so. Rossana Cottage lay empty, waiting for an event that never took place. She knew that her own behaviour had contributed to his leaving her for periods of time to make his own life without her. Perhaps it was grief

LEFT: *Figures carved on the pillar of the harp.*
RIGHT: *Inscription: Sebastian Erard, 18 Great Marlborough Street*

also for the lost love of her youth, for the 'T. Singleton' mentioned in her cousin's memoir, for the shock of realising she was not strong enough to say 'no' to Henry Tighe's proposal. And for William, who as a very young man had danced with her at Dublin Castle, whose generosity allowed him to include her in his happy family life, whose tenderness inspired her to understand what she lacked; William, a landlord who lived at home for the main part, unlike many of his contemporaries and was trusted by his tenants, an MP who worked tirelessly to get through a bill which stipulated that a jury should be half Catholic when Catholics were tried. Her grief was love for William, who was hers in blood, but not her own, and for Harry, who was hers, but whom she had never really claimed.

Her novel *Selena* gives interesting insights into her preoccupations and her nature. Her 'secret grief' is in some way hidden in this long work which she wrote alongside 'Psyche; or, The Legend of Love' from 1801 to 1803, where she deals more openly with her experience of life and the failings of society. All kinds of sensuality are portrayed: cheating, violent behaviour, adultery, unwanted pregnancy and attempted suicide. First cousins are coerced into marriages they do not wish to make and adults betray the young with alarming self-interest and dexterity. Tuberculosis plays a significant part, alighting, with sleight of hand, perhaps, upon the heroine's mother rather than upon Selena herself. Men behave badly and women too, some, like Lady Harriet Modely, with no other thought in their head but the fashion of the moment.

Cousin Caroline comments that Mary began without knowing how she would end her novel *Selena*, 'unlike Miss Edgeworth, who I remember told me that she generally finished the entire rough sketch of her story before she filled it up'. It is clear that Caroline Hamilton knew Edgeworth well and was influenced by her, for her own sketches and drawings of the period have the novelist's satirical edge. *Selena* gives no such commentary on the political events of the time, but is rather a social romance with bearing on Mary Tighe's preoccupations.

*Selena* is the story of a young, talented and beautiful woman who sets out into the fashionable world at seventeen with very little guidance from her parents. Her father has quarrelled violently with his brother and uses his daughter unscrupulously to take revenge. Her mother dies at a critical moment of 'a rapid consumption': Selena is alone in the world of eighteenth-century society with all its attendant immorality and unreliable suitors. In Chapter Three she plays and sings for her cousin Lord Dallamore 'who was as much pleased as his indolent and unenjoying disposition ever allowed him to feel'. Mrs Vallard, her mother's best friend and her godmother, who looks after her at this time, considers him remarkably clever, but a firm authorial voice promptly enters the text: 'We must however in some degree differ from his partial aunt. Lord Dallamore was not clever.'

As the novel progresses, Dallamore is revealed as a lazy and undistinguished young man about town with little capacity to form a loving relationship, although from time to time he tries. It is tempting here to see references to Henry Tighe who also fell for his first cousin. A central portrait sympathetically drawn is of young Emily Montrose who has been married off to Lord Trevallyn while being in love with Lord Henry Ortney. Lady Trevallyn has obeyed her mother's wishes for a safe marriage and is trapped in a loveless union with a much older man. The characters develop a little in a somewhat melodramatic manner and in a roundabout of doubtful liaisons in gothic settings. Some of the poems which are brought into the various love stories in the plot suggest Mary Tighe's personal experience.

Selena finds a poem, 'Fled are the Summer Hours of Joy and Love' in a botany book. It was written by Lady Trevallyn the summer before she married and tells of her love for Lord Henry Ortney:

*Oft when my heart the call of joy would spurn*
*By sad involuntary gloom opprest,*
*To thee my plaintive harp I languid turn*
*The silver sounds can sooth my soul to rest –*
*Or wrapt in loved imagination's dream*
*I hear the voice, I see the form so dear,*
*In visionary charms they present seem*
*The well known accents vibrate on mine ear –*
*I see those eyes of bright celestial blue,*
*Those laughing eyes beam love and sympathy,*
*And o'er the mantling cheek the rosy hue*
*The blush of kindling hope and tender joy –*
*I have not lost thee then, my soul's best part!*
*I still can hear thee talk of love and bliss!*
*Can pour out all the fullness of my heart,*
*Oh what felicity can vie with this!*[3]

The subject matter here is unfulfilled early love, which is assuaged by playing the harp and turning over memories of the beloved. This and many other poems in the novel have a melancholy touch which springs from personal experience.

The novel is a critique of the fashionable manners of the day. There is much reported speech and few dramatic scenes with dialogue; many gothic, mysterious and unexplained beatings of the heart are alternated with comment on the 'ton'. The character of Selena's father is exaggeratedly evil and has none of the redeeming features of Jane Austen's General Tilney. It is tempting to imagine that the paths of Jane Austen and Mary Tighe might have crossed at Bath.

Nonetheless, the novel has its virtues and the quotations at the beginning of each chapter of *Selena* are an indication of the range of the author's reading and understanding: Charlotte Smith, Lady Mary Wortley Montagu,

James Beattie, Jane Porter, Anna Seward, Joanna Baillie, Hannah More, Shakespeare, Milton, Dryden, Petrarch and Beaumont and Fletcher are amongst those cited. There are sharp insights into the relationships between characters in the story and an implied criticism of an older generation whose worldly concerns overwhelm their natural feeling for their offspring. The lack of structure to the novel as a whole is in marked contrast to the meticulously worked poem 'Psyche; or, The Legend of Love' and the discriminating philosophy put forward there. Perhaps the discipline of writing 'Psyche' demanded the relief of creating a loosely woven story that might be revised later. Selena's story ends in her marriage to the man who truly loves her, Sidney Dallamore, who is her cousin and the cousin of Lord Dallamore, who eventually releases her: there must surely be an element of wish-fulfilment in this denouement. Whereas in Psyche's journey through the 'mazy' wood, the challenges of life are presented allegorically, Selina's hurdles on the course to happiness are woven into the structure of the novel in various characters and counterpointed themes. Her good nature, her tenacity and growing knowledge of what is valuable in life inform the novel and bring her to happiness. Selena, Psyche and Mary have much in common.

Mary's grief was a cry from the hidden part of her heart. William turned towards her and proffered his hand to help in practical ways; he gave financial security and a place to spend her last days. She had a refuge, gardens to enjoy and she found a kindred spirit to sit beside on the lawns at Woodstock on the rare occasions when parliamentary duties in London allowed him to be at home. Here was one who wrote poetry himself and who was prepared to read, to advise on her work; they sat together working and talking, or in companionable silence. Mary's mind was still sharply alert. Harry could come and go as he pleased and William and Marianne made her feel part of the wider family. Her maid Caroline was always to hand for her physical needs, as well as her mother, whose presence to the end gave a mixture of pain and pleasure.

To drive out in the carriage was always the greatest joy and it may have been her final outing that brought on the fatal illness. Two weeks before her cousin died, Caroline Hamilton had written her last letter to Mary:

My dearest Mary, It gives me the greatest pleasure to hear that you suffer less and we trust that your Mama's next letter will confirm a still better account of you, though we cannot help thinking that you were a little venturesome in driving out so early in the year.[4]

Caroline goes on tell her the local news and ends with the words: 'Mama sends her very best love. I need not say that we think of you continually and watch with the greater anxiety for a letter from Woodstock.'

This final unwise drive was perhaps a last bid for freedom and independence on the part of a still young writer who loved the garden in the spring and who was perhaps overwhelmed by the painful kindness of those around her, yet completely powerless to change what was happening. Her instinct said that Mr Innis's blister was taking away her last vestige of strength but bloodletting was routine, despite the protest of many a patient. She was very weak. Opiates brought little relief to failing strength and agonising pain. She had been ill for many years and her relationships with others had long been conditioned by her illness. William and Marianne had generously given her the main living room for her bedroom now they were in London and her capacity for writing comes almost to a close, with a few significant exceptions.

She looked back at the poems she had written about death from the time she started writing. At first for Mary, dying was something that happened to other people. But the poems of her middle years express pure fear after the diagnosis of consumption. The last group turns from death and physical suffering to life, the life she loved so dearly and knew she must soon leave.

In 1801 Mary was twenty-nine years old and there was no longer any doubt about *that fatal day*. With a humility bred of sickness, she assessed her life's failures and saw herself as having been deluded in her hopes:

> *As nearer I approach that fatal day*
> *Which makes all mortal cares appear so light,*
> *Time seems on swifter wing to speed his flight,*
> *And hope's fallacious visions fade away;*
> *While to my fond desires, at length, I say,*

*Behold how quickly melted from your sight*
*The promised objects you esteemed so bright,*
*When love was all your song and life looked gay!*
*Now let us rest in peace! Those hours are past,*
*And with them all, the agitating train*
*By which hope led the wandering cheated soul;*
*Wearied, she seeks repose, and owns at last*
*How sighs, and tears, and youth were spent in vain,*
*While languishing she mourned in folly's sad control.*[5]

By December 1804 her poems take on a new tone, less reflective, more direct, acknowledging the physical pain of illness with new humility, recognising the need for friends:

*But I, poor sufferer, doomed in vain*
*To woo the health which Heaven denied,*
*Though nights of horror, nights of pain*
*The baffled opiate's force deride,*

*Yet well I know, and grateful feel,*
*How much can lenient kindness do*
*From anguish half its darts to steal*
*And faded hope's sick smile renew.*[6]

In pure despair, Mary writes her own version of Psalm 130 in January 1805:

*From sorrow's depths to thee I cry,*
*O thou, who knowest my inmost fear,*
*The unuttered prayer, the half-breathed sigh,*
*Still let it reach thy pitying ear.*[7]

From 1805 to 1810 the subject matter of the poetry changes again. No longer concerned with the horror of death because she has come to terms with her illness, she turns instead to life itself. But it is interesting and significant that she wrote only one poem which refers to the death of her father which took place when she was an infant. The poem is about a myrtle planted by her aunt to celebrate the birth of her niece. She writes of her namesake, Mary Blachford, sister to her father, who planted the myrtle on the day the poet was born many years ago. She did this,

> *. . . that the plant, thus reared in future years*
> *Might win his smile benignant, when her hand*
> *Should point where, in its bower of loveliness,*
> *Bright spreading to the sun its fragrant leaf,*
> *His Mary's myrtle bloomed – Ah me! 'tis sad*
> *When sweet affection thus designs in vain,*
> *And sees the fragile web it smiling spun*
> *In playful love, crushed by the sudden storm,*
> *And swept to dark oblivion mid the wreck*
> *Of greater hopes! – Even while she thought of bliss,*
> *Already o'er that darling brother's head*
> *The death-commissioned angel noiseless waved*
> *His black and heavy wings . . .*[8]

The 'death-commissioned angel' has come for her father and will soon take him away. The angel is noiseless and his 'black and heavy wings' will haunt William Blachford's daughter with increasing intensity.

'The Lily' was written in May 1809 just as Mary set out for Woodstock to be with those she loved. This is one of her final poems and the mood is no longer angry; rather, she feels awed as she understands that she herself is part of a much greater cycle.

> *How withered, perished seems the form*
> *Of yon obscure, unsightly root!*
> *Yet from the blight of wintry storm,*
> *It hides secure the precious fruit.*
>
> *The careless eye can find no grace,*
> *No beauty in the scaly folds,*
> *Nor see within the dark embrace*
> *What latent loveliness it holds.*
>
> *Yet in that bulb, those sapless scales,*
> *The lily wraps her silver vest,*
> *Till vernal suns and vernal gales*
> *Shall kiss once more her fragrant breast.*

*Yes, hide beneath the mouldering heap*
*The undelighting, slighted thing:*
*There in the cold earth buried deep,*
*In silence let it wait the spring.*

Mary vividly describes the shrivelled lily root and then evokes the mysterious power which translates the 'scaly folds' into a flower of great beauty.

*And thou, O virgin Queen of Spring!*
*Shalt, from thy dark and lowly bed,*
*Bursting thy green sheath's silken string,*
*Unveil thy charms and perfume shed;*

*Unfold thy robes of purest white,*
*Unsullied from their darksome grave,*
*And thy soft petals silvery light*
*In the mild breeze unfettered wave . . .*

'The Lily' captures Mary's keen awareness of the natural cycle of death and rebirth. The 'scaly folds' of the lily and the 'dark embrace' of the earth are acknowledged with simplicity and without fear. The last verse of the poem is a statement of faith: she like the lily will...

*. . . bear the long, cold wintry night,*
*And bear her own degraded doom,*
*And wait till Heaven's reviving light;*
*Eternal Spring! Shall burst the gloom.*[9]

NOTES

1 Theodosia Blachford: *Observations on the Journal of Mary Tighe*, NLI 4810.
2 'Address to my Harp', 1805.
3 'Fled are the Summer Hours of Joy and Love' from *Selena*.
4 Letter from Caroline Hamilton to Mary Tighe, 7 March 1810, PRONI.
5 Sonnet: 'As nearer I approach that fatal day', written November 1801.
6 'Verses Written in Sickness', December 1804.
7 'From Sorrow's Depths', December 1805.
8 'Written at West-Aston', June 1808.
9 'The Lily', May 1809.

# CHAPTER 14

# AT WOODSTOCK
## *'May in vain'*

Two weeks after arriving at Woodstock, Mary wrote a sonnet asking the muse who inspired her cousin as he walked in his fine gardens to come also to her. William too suffered 'the soul-subduing powers of mortal ill' and he had endured an acute asthma attack in the months before Mary's arrival.

> *Sweet pious muse! Whose chastely graceful form*
> *Delighted oft amid these shades to stray,*
> *To their loved master breathing many a lay*
> *Divinely soothing; oh! be near to charm*
> *For me the languid hours of pain, and warm*
> *This heart depressed with one aspiring ray*
> *From such bright visions as were wont to play*
> *Around his favoured brow, when, to disarm*
> *The soul-subduing powers of mortal ill,*
> *Thy soft voice lured him 'to his ivied seat',*
> *'His classic roses' or his 'healthy hill';*
> *Or by yon trickling fount delayed his feet*
> *Beneath his own dear oaks, when present still,*
> *The melodies of Heaven thou didst unseen repeat.*[1]

The elegant, measured style of the sonnet at first gives little away: 'his favoured brow' is as near as we get to William's physical presence. But the tone is calm and Mary is confident that she will find peace of mind in these grounds that he has cherished with love. His presence informs the poem.

*Gardening at Woodstock*

On 24 June 1809 Theodosia arrived at Woodstock to take care of her daughter. She wrote an account of Mary's last months:

> How often have I thought when gazing at my poor child's dejected countenance, faded beauty, blasted hopes and vain pursuits, how the thoughts that oppressed my heart if well expressed 'Would point a moral and adorn a tale'. I am very inadequate to the expression of them nor have I any female child, nor grandchild, to whom I can hope that they may be useful yet, after inspecting all her journals & papers, I feel a desire to leave some account of God's judgements on myself, through her, and of that Mercy which endureth for ever.[2]

While it is easy to sympathise with Theodosia's shock at the 'dejected countenance' of her daughter, her 'faded beauty' and her 'blasted hopes', it is nonetheless very difficult to see the writing and publication of *Psyche* as anything less than a superb achievement, yet she could not fully allow such praise for her child. Caroline Hamilton writes in her journal that Theodosia 'had the satisfaction of seeing her daughter removed from the flattering society which she considered so injurious to her'. She clearly did not approve of the literary afternoons held at Dominick Street, and her attitude to her daughter's worldly behaviour colours her judgement at many points in the narrative of her death. It is significant that Theodosia quotes from Samuel Johnson's 'The Vanity of Human Wishes', the very title of which sums up her attitude to life. Mother and daughter had seldom been apart. There were stresses between them from the time when Mary was a very promising child and Theodosia a single parent. Their relationship was often uneasy when Mary was a girl and the strain did not ease when she was a young woman sick with consumption and married to a man she had to learn to love. Yet overall, Theodosia's tenderness, dedication and honesty shine from her account. Mother suffered at every step with daughter and was not protected either by Harry or John from the exigencies of the sick room: she had to manage as best she could: 'On 24 [June 1809] I joined them at Woodstock. But Oh what did I feel when I leaned forward to kiss her as she held out her hand to draw me to her, I saw evidently the hand of death stamped upon her face, and was, from that moment, persuaded that she never could leave Woodstock but in her coffin; yet – we talked and smiled and seemed chearful [*sic*].'[3]

There was a brief interlude during which the patient, for that is what she now was, went out in the carriage or sometimes on horseback led by the servant and she was able to enjoy the new and improved delights of the flourishing estate and seek the inspiration of Woodstock described in her sonnet to William. But on 7 August, while Henry was attending the Assizes of Kilkenny, Mary was seized 'with this great and deadly illness'. It is clear that Theodosia does not really understand the nature of the disease. She goes on to say she believes that it was gout or rheumatism in the stomach:

> . . . I believe that not one of her many Physicians ever knew the real cause of her sufferings (her extraordinary sufferings) tho I suppose it is too certain that the fatal illness she had in December 1800 laid the foundation of them. We now thought her hour was indeed come but it pleased God to prolong her life for more than seven months. After this attack she lived in great solitude, seeing no one but Harry, her faithful maid Caroline and myself

and occasionally Mr Innis. Her brother during this period paid her three visits and by his desire, to her great comfort, Mr Richards came to her at an early period of her illness – her patience, gentleness and kindness were great – her bodily sufferings were not all she had to contend with, but whatever she could not remedy she suffered silently and was very grateful for every instance of attention and kindness which indeed she met with from every individual of the family.[4]

The 'attention and kindness from every individual of the family' includes William. Harry did his his best and read cheerfully to his dying wife while trying not to argue with his mother-in-law. Theodosia writes: '. . . but when Harry was present, he or I read something of an amusing kind, as she thought that anything not really evil was to be preferred to our sitting staring at her, or perhaps, disputing as we were certainly not of one mind, tho' I bless God, that I ever loved him, not have any reason to doubt his affectionate regard for me.'

About this time, December 1809, Mary was taken ill. 'She was seized with a faintness, apparently the faintness of death,' Theodosia recounts. Pen and paper were called for and two and a half pages were written which Theodosia was ordered to give to Harry after her death. At the same time she asked 'dearest Mama' to take 'the trouble and sorrow of looking over my papers' and in this letter she bequeathed to her brother fifty volumes, requesting him to write in them these words: 'From my only sister, from her to whom I was most dear from infancy to death'. She provided for her maid, Caroline, and went on to address Harry 'with a trembling hand but legible':

Generous, dearest love! Do not mind anything else I may have left, but I promised kind Caroline she should never want and you will fulfill my promise – my beloved! My last hours have been comforted by your tenderness and only embittered by the grief that I have not been to you such as you deserved – Oh! Take care of yourself, and do not let mistaken generosity lead you to hurt yourself for ever in Society. Adieu, but not for ever, we shall meet above –[5]

The core of their relationship is revived in this last telling letter. Mary recognises Harry's natural generosity of spirit and acknowledges their shortcomings as having been hers as much as his, if not more. She warns him against 'mistaken generosity', a sharp and telling phrase that draws attention to his lack of worldly astuteness. She grieves that there is now no time to make amends for an imperfect relationship, which is warmed in its final moments by the childlike affection that brought them together in the first place. Their childlessness, their restless wanderings she now acknowledges to be partly her fault.

*Winter-flowering daphne, or mezereon*

'On Receiving a Branch of Mezereon' is one of the most important poems in the story of Mary Tighe. At Woodstock in December 1809 someone brought in from the garden a flowering branch of mezereon or daphne, a kind of laurel that sometimes blooms in the very heart of winter at Christmas-time even in snow, and is regarded as a harbinger of spring. Pinkish, pungent, it flowers unexpectedly on the branch before the leaf arrives. Mary Tighe thinks of the coming year but knows that she will not see May:

> *Odours of Spring, my sense ye charm*
> *With fragrance premature;*
> *And mid these days of dark alarm,*
> *Almost to hope allure.*
> *Methinks with purpose soft ye come*
> *To tell of brighter hours,*
> *Of May's blue skies, abundant bloom,*
> *Her sunny gales and showers.*
>
> *Alas! For me shall May in vain*
> *The powers of life restore;*
> *These eyes that weep and watch in pain*
> *Shall see her charms no more.*
> *No, no, this anguish cannot last!*
> *Beloved friends adieu!*
> *The bitterness of death were past*
> *Could I resign but you.*
>
> *But oh! in every mortal pang*
> *That rends my soul from life,*
> *That soul which seems on you to hang*
> *Through each convulsive strife,*
> *Even now, with agonizing grasp*
> *Of terror and regret,*
> *To all in life its love would clasp*
> *Clings close and closer yet.*

Then the poet turns to address her friends and family. Those close to her are gathered around her – they 'sooth the pangs of death'.

*Oh ye! who sooth the pangs of death*
*With love's own patient care,*
*Still, still retain this fleeting breath,*
*Still pour the fervent prayer:-*
*And ye, whose smile must greet my eye*
*No more, nor voice my ear,*
*Who breathe for me the tender sigh,*
*And shed the pitying tear,*

*Whose kindness (though far far removed)*
*My grateful thoughts perceive,*
*Pride of my life, esteemed, beloved,*
*My last sad claim receive!*
*Oh! do not quite your friend forget,*
*Forget alone her faults;*
*And speak of her with fond regret*
*Who asks your lingering thoughts.*[6]

The last two verses include an address to William. She knew she would not see him again – 'And ye, whose smile must greet my eye/No more'. He is 'far, far removed'. William is the 'pride of my life, esteemed, beloved' to whom she makes her 'last sad claim'? She asks him to 'speak of her with fond regret'. This he will do in response to this poem, the very last that she will write, with his own verses on the walls of her mausoleum at Inistioge after her death.

Psyche's journey through the mazy wood was nearly over. Life was not to be as neat as art, and Mary found that Cupid had a compound presence in her last days. Her affection for Harry revived in the face of death because he stayed by her and tenderly sustained her, despite the vagaries of their past relationship. The protective affection of his brother William had provided for all her material as well as many of her writerly needs and reassured her that to have loved was enough. Her mother stood by her as she always had done, quietly unassuming, concerned with both body and soul, caring despite all odds. Her maid Caroline tended to her every need. And John, her brother, whom she

– 208 –

had loved for so long, was there to comfort her. In addition to these five, others such as Marianne Tighe and Caroline Hamilton were close in spirit too.

There was worse to come. Mary became 'dropsical', that is to say her body retained water, particularly the legs and feet. Mr Richards, her Dublin doctor, gave up hope for her: 'With a sad look and a tear she threw his letter on the couch and said, "He gives me up".' Mr Innis was called to attend and gave Mary the benefit of his care since her feet had become 'decidedly mortified'.

That the practices of medicine in this period of the nineteenth century were sometimes life-threatening is undoubtedly true. Blistering or cupping (the drawing of blood) would in fact have deprived Mary of her last ounces of strength, yet such treatment was still firmly accepted by the general public, even though the effects of a session had deleterious effects. It did not disappear from British medicine until the late nineteenth century and was routine to such an extent that patients would simply not have questioned its use even in the very late stages of a mortal illness. In her account of her husband's last days, Theodosia writes that on the last evening William Blachford was still up, in July 1773, 'he had sent for a surgeon who bled him white'.[7] He retired to bed and died soon after. The first of the cuppings given within a few days of Mary's death would have made her visibly weaker, the second probably killed her. Her mother was right in saying '…I believe that not one of her many Physicians ever knew the real cause of her sufferings (her extraordinary sufferings)'.

Early on in March 1810, '…at her earnest request, the weather being very mild for the season, she was out three times round the lawn, in a carriage, but she looked so faint and ghastly that it was to me a very sad and mournful spectacle. Nor could I consider it as proof of her amendment.'[8] It was on 21 March that Mary left her room so that it could be cleaned and went into the dining room. This was the day brother John arrived about one o'clock in the afternoon and she seemed particularly delighted and revived to see him. The fire was low, there were draughts coming in through the windows but despite her mother's entreaties, she would not put on more clothes. This sad little argument about keeping warm, 'putting that shawl on', had taken place so many times between them, and on this day Mary still reacted as she had when she was a girl – she left it off: 'My poor dear love was I am sure tired by my over-solicitude for all her interests, temporal and spiritual and, like all other sins, it brought to me its own punishment.'[9]

Mary caught cold as she sat in the draughty Woodstock drawing room and by the next day she was very poorly indeed. She summoned her brother and her husband and told them that though for many months she had been afraid of dying, she now felt her fear lift. Her face lit up as she said these words. John, who had sat with her in the earlier days of her illness whenever she asked him to do so, noticed the change in her demeanour. Later that evening Mr Innis applied his first blister, thereby almost certainly precluding any hope for Mary of seeing the spring come in. But neither Mr Innis nor Mary's relations knew this for a fact. They all stayed close to her and the next day passed without Theodosia being able to remember what happened.

It was the next night, Friday, that was the last. Innis stayed in the house all night and in the evening put another blister on. The pathos is shared equally between mother and daughter in the following scene:

> In the course of the evening she gave me so sweet and kind a farewell kiss as I can never forget. It seemed to say, what will you do without me? & frequently warmed her poor cold face on mine. Once she put her death cold hands in my bosom from the dreadful feel of which I involuntarily shrunk. Oh why did I not rather press them to my heart?[10]

Mary was given half a grain of opium and lay quietly and allowed her mother to be in the room with her. 'I would rather you stayed' were the last words she addressed to Theodosia. During the first part of the night she slept comparatively easily and then the nurse brought her the yolk of an egg. Caroline says, 'she retained the perfect use of her faculties to her very last breath'. Mary took the cup in her hand and swallowed the egg and then gave directions for the carman who was to go to Kilkenny the following morning. But soon after she called Innis. He took her pulse, and called the men to her, but before Harry and John could get to her room she had died. It was 2.00 a.m. on Saturday 24 March 1810.

For three and a half days her body was kept at Woodstock 'looking far better, fairer and younger than she had done for many months before,' so Theodosia said, and she would not allow the coffin to be closed until Innis declared that it must be done: 'So ended my dream of thirty-seven years continuance, filled with bright hope's vain elation, wasting anxieties and cruel anguish. Indeed, I do not think there is any passion my heart is capable of feeling which was not by her exercised to the utmost.'

Theodosia's life-work was her daughter, for better or worse. His heart warmed by Mary's tender farewell to him, Henry rose to the occasion and his tribute was to edit an edition of *Psyche, with Other Poems* for Longmans to publish in 1811. And at the end of her account, Theodosia speaks of 'a new tomb [at Inistioge] where HT intends to have some memorial of her'. Henry commissioned John Flaxman to sculpt a reclining figure (on which he never completed the payments) and made arrangements for the mausoleum to be built. Considerably later, probably well after the death of William in 1816, and of Theodosia and John Blachford in 1817, the stone figure was installed on the tomb and the engravings set in the walls. And William's poem was added below, surrounding her with praise – and with the respect he had never been able fully to express in his lifetime for fear of damaging further the relationships which were so closely entwined by blood.

May came in vain at Woodstock for there was no brave lover of spring to venture out too daringly in a carriage or on horseback to see the many-arched bridge over the Nore and the rolling hills of Kilkenny.

NOTES

1 Sonnet: 'Written at Woodstock in the County of Kilkenny, the Seat of William Tighe', 30 June 1809.
2 Theodosia Blachford: *Observations on the Journal of Mary Tighe*, NLI 4810.
3 ibid.
4 ibid.
5 ibid.

6  'On Receiving a Branch of Mezereon, which flowered at Woodstock', December 1809.

7  *Some memorandums of the death of Mrs Blachford's husband written by herself,* 11 May 1773 NLI  4810.

8  Theodosia Blachford: *Observations on the Journal of Mary Tighe*, NLI  4810.

9  ibid.

10  ibid.

# CHAPTER 15

# TRIBUTES

*'Thou art not lost'*

At Inistioge churchyard lies the effigy of Mary Tighe by John Flaxman inside a four-square neo-classical tomb of mature stone. The grass is long in the churchyard in this secluded part of the village and the ruins of an old abbey stand nearby. A little winged figure perches lightly on her shoulder looking down at her pensive face. Is this the Genius

*Detail of the figure at Mary's shoulder on her tomb*

of Poetry as some commentators have assumed, or perhaps the figure of Psyche? Many of Flaxman's monuments have guardian angels and he was known as a man of strong religious belief who was influenced by the transcendent spirituality of the Swedenborgian movement and, like the poet William Blake, was against the rationalism of the Church of England. Swedenborg believed that at death man regenerated into a spiritual being and took on angelic form. Angels guard and protect the living. Such imagery allowed a kind of non-conformist spirituality to exist within the Church of England and this would have appealed to the Methodist Tighe family.

Flaxman's account book records Henry Tighe as commissioning a monumental statue in 1814 of Mrs Tighe, to cost a hundred guineas, £20 paid on account. The statue was exhibited in London at The Royal Academy in the summer of 1815 and there are two plaster models, one owned by University College, London, and the other by the Tighe family (now at Rothe House, Kilkenny). Neither of the models has the figure on the shoulder of the poet. Perhaps it was added afterwards and made by another hand. But according to the catalogue of a Christie's sale of 1856, the figure was adapted from the *Psyche* made by Flaxman for Samuel Rogers, the model of which is in the Sir John Soane's Museum in London.

In the year after Mary's death, 1811, Henry Tighe saw to the publication with Longmans of *Psyche, with Other Poems* (the first public edition) and this was intended as a tribute to his wife – who had herself refused the opportunity to publish with a firm such as Longmans and had chosen instead a private printing of fifty copies for friends. Many years before when the newly married couple first went to London, Harry had enjoyed showing his wife in society. And now after her death he looked forward to enjoying the public tributes which he knew would come with multiple editions, as well as profitable remuneration, some of which was to go to the House of Refuge in Dublin, Theodosia's charity for women. William was not one to pass comments unless they were asked for, but when Henry suggested publishing *Selena*, he was cautious. William had read the long novel and pointed out that Mary had wanted to make revisions. William himself had listed suggestions for her on one of their long working days at Woodstock in her last year. A *Reading Journal* entry for 1809 reads 'WT's objections to *Selena*'[1] and lists many points for revision. So Henry waited. But after William died in August 1817, followed closely by Theodosia in November of the same year, he contacted Longmans again and they were keen to start preparation immediately. But *Selena* was not published. That Henry changed his mind is curious. Perhaps he read further in the novel than he had done earlier and detected the uncanny resonance of the unhappy union of a young woman with a first cousin, a marriage into which she slips because she has not the will-power to refuse (and hurt) him; a marriage which is never fulfilled.

There were many others who missed Mary Tighe, and many paid tribute, notably the poet Thomas Moore, who had cheerfully bustled in to visit her on the couch at Dominick Street in the earlier days of her illness and who shared her love of writing above all else; and Felicia Hemans, who had never met her but who was influenced by her work. Much later, in 1831 Hemans travelled to Kilkenny to see the tomb in the country churchyard and wrote three poems on the subject.

Thomas Moore was seven years younger than Mary Tighe. Her life and its painful end clearly affected him, as is revealed in the poem he wrote shortly after her death, published in 1811:

> *I saw thy form in youthful prime,*
> *Nor thought that pale decay*
> *Would steal before the steps of Time,*
> *And waste its bloom away, Mary!*
> *Yet still thy features wore that light,*
> *Which fleets not with the breath;*
> *And life ne'er looked more truly bright*
> *Than in thy smile of death, Mary![2]*

They had had in common a certain early bloom. The 'pale decay', which had lately affected Mary's still youthful form, frightened Moore deeply. Yet when she died, he found a way of remembering with a lyrical tribute the modest manner that hid a streak of poetic gold:

> *As streams that run o'er golden mines,*
> *Yet humbly, calmly glide,*
> *Nor seem to know the wealth that shines*
> *Within their gentle tide, Mary!*
> *So veil'd beneath the simplest guise,*
> *Thy radiant genius shone,*
> *And that, which charm'd all other eyes,*
> *Seem'd worthless in thy own, Mary!*
>
> *If souls could always dwell above,*
> *Thou ne'er hadst left that sphere;*
> *Or could we keep the souls we love,*
> *We ne'er had lost thee here, Mary!*
> *Though many a gifted mind we meet,*
> *Though fairest forms we see,*
> *To live with them is far less sweet,*
> *Than to remember thee, Mary!*

The tributes paid by Felicia Hemans (1793–1835) are equally appreciative. She herself showed early talent and published her first poem at fifteen. She married and had five sons but her husband left to go to his home in Italy and never returned, whereafter she kept her family through her writing. When Mary Tighe died, she wrote a poem in which she imagined going to see the tomb 'without the slightest idea of ever visiting it':

> *I stood beside thy lowly grave;*
> *Spring-odours breathed around,*
> *And music, in the river-wave,*
> *Pass'd with a lulling sound.*[3]

But it was not until 1831 that Felicia actually visited Inistioge and saw the tomb in the mausoleum:

I wish to give you an account of an interesting day I lately passed, before its images become faint in my recollection. We went to Woodstock, the place where the late Mrs Tighe, whose poetry has always been very touching to my feelings, passed the latest years of her life, and near which she is buried. The scenery of the place is magnificent, the style of which I think I prefer to every other; wild profound glens, rich with every hue and form of foliage, and a rapid river sweeping through them, now lost and now lighting up the deep woods with sudden flashes of its waves…I should have told you that Woodstock is now the seat of Lady Louisa Tighe. Amongst other persons of the party was Mr Henry Tighe, the widower of the poetess. He had just been exercising one of his accomplishments in the translation into Latin of a little poem of mine: and I am told that his version is very elegant. We went to the tomb, 'the grave of a poetess' where there is a monument by Flaxman: it consists of a recumbent female figure, with much of the repose, the mysterious sweetness of happy death, which to me is so affecting in monumental sculpture.[4]

It is interesting to see that Henry Tighe is still exercising his charms upon lady writers and finding his Latin handy. Felicia Hemans goes on in the same letter to say that,

This place of rest made me very thoughtful; I could not but reflect on the many changes which had brought me to the spot I had commemorated three years since, without the slightest idea of ever visiting it; and though surrounded by attention and the appearance of interest, my heart was envying the repose of her who slept there.[5]

There was a second poem about Mary Tighe, 'Written after visiting a tomb, near Woodstock, in the County of Kilkenny'. The lines come alive with her evocation of place and she opens with a quotation from Mary's poem, 'The Lily':

> Yes! Hide beneath the mouldering heap,
> The undelighting, slighted thing;
> There in the cold earth, buried deep,
> In silence let it wait the Spring.

> *I stood where the lip of song lay low,*
> *Where the dust had gathered on Beauty's brow;*
> *Where stillness lay on the heart of Love*
> *And a marble weeper kept watch above.*

She describes how she saw a butterfly 'flitting past that solemn tomb/ Over a bright world of joy and bloom' and thought of all the things that separated her own life from the creature 'winged and free':

*Yet e'er I turned from that silent place,*
*Or ceased from watching thy sunny race,*
*Thou, even thou, on those glancing wings,*
*Didst waft me with visions of brighter things!*

*Thou that dost image the freed soul's birth,*
*And its flight away o'er the mists of earth,*
*Oh! Fitly thy path is through flowers that rise*
*Round the dark chamber where Genius lies.*[6]

Only one poem by Hemans is remembered today, 'Casablanca', or 'The Boy Stood on the Burning Deck' which tells the powerful if pathetic story of a boy transfixed by his sense of duty in his position upon the burning deck of a ship in the Peninsular War, a doomed ship, in the bowels of which the boy's father lies dying. Our hero will not surrender his position or his pride until his father gives the word for him to go. That permission never comes. Felicia's soldier brothers, her husband and five young sons enabled her vicariously to widen her sphere of interest in the world as the British Empire grew and to write in a popular manner of men's experience in a way that Mary Tighe did not achieve, despite the fact that she lived and wrote through the Napoleonic wars, which get only a sideways glance in her work.

Mary and Felicia had several things in common: their private unhappiness about their personal lives, which could not be openly discussed, a love of poetry and a gift for expression, which was remarkable in both women. But Mary's life intrigued the younger woman, who returned to the subject of her death in a third poem. Felicia had been to visit Rossana where Mary had written 'Psyche; or, The Legend of Love' in the attic room so many years before.

*Lines Written for the Album at Rossana*

*Oh! Lightly tread through these deep chestnut-bowers*
*Where a sweet spirit once in beauty moved!*
*And touch with reverent hands these leaves and flowers,*
*Fair things, which well a gentle heart hath loved!*
*A gentle heart, of love and grief the abode,*
*Whence the bright streams of song in tear-drops flow'd.*

> *And bid its memory sanctify the scene!*
> *And let the ideal presence of the dead*
> *Float round, and touch the woods with softer green,*
> *And o'er the streams a charm, like moonlight, shed;*
> *Through the soul's depths in holy silence felt –*
> *A spell to raise, to chasten and to melt!*[7]

Felicia Hemans had come to Rossana to pay homage to a poet and to a woman whose 'secret grief' touched her profoundly. Her poem stands as evidence of Mary Tighe's contribution not just to the body of poetry written by eighteenth and early nineteenth-century women poets, but also as testimony to the way in which she represented the captive lives of women caught in a social system that gave them little chance to blossom, who turned to writing for greater freedom of expression.

Mary's cousin Caroline Hamilton returned to Rossana after her cousin's death and slept in the bow-room at Rossana where 'Psyche' had been written. Touchingly she speaks of Mary in a poem she herself wrote in the same high room:

> *On this dear lawn beneath that spreading lime*
> *I think I see thee in thy beauty's prime,*
> *My long-lost friend, and till I cease to be,*
> *How can I, Mary, not remember thee?*
> *Thy sparkling eyes are still to memory dear,*
> *Thy accents mild still vibrate in my ear.*
> *Alas I saw thee hurried through each stage,*
> *From blooming youth to premature old age;*
> *The room I now inhabit, once was thine;*
> *Thy couch thy table, and thy bed are mine;*
> *And oft when gazing on thy favourite chair,*
> *Wak'd by the moon's pale light, I see thee there,*
> *Tracing thy Psyche's long and tedious way*
> *Through gloomy paths to realms of brightest day.*[8]

Mary had no sister and she was particularly close to Caroline, who was her husband's sister and therefore her sister-in-law, but also her first cousin: their close relationship was bound by blood and by marriage in a manner characteristic of this time and culture. As well as being a tender memorial to Mary, the poem is a lament for a great house which is no longer vibrant with life:

> *Oh, how this house is changed since thou wast here:*
> *The sound of mirth no more salutes mine ear.*
> *Much valued friends and dear relations came*
> *To meet together here, their tastes the same;*
> *Collected round the fire, each strove who best*
> *Should tell the merry tale or point the jest.*
> *The grave, the gay, by turns our thoughts employed,*
> *And every moment was alike enjoyed.*

Caroline went back to her home at Hamwood House, tired by her grief for Mary but glad to have mourned her loss in the house they both loved so much.

Theodosia made a special final tribute to her daughter with the private publication of a number of copies in late 1811 of *Mary, A Series of Reflections During Twenty Years*, which in its modest character (thirty-five small pages, some hand-written) may be seen as a response to Henry's lavish publication of *Psyche, with Other Poems* with Longmans in May 1811. *Reflections* was to be distributed to a few friends 'for whom *alone* this selection was intended'. Although her name is not inscribed anywhere on this manuscript, several signs tell us that it is Theodosia's work: the poems are all related to Mary's spiritual state – 'Happy is he whose thoughtful mind/Seeks contentment not on earth', 'These charms which now I blush to own . . .', 'Poem on Good Friday' – Theodosia selects those aspects of her daughter's poetry which suit her own religious persuasion. Her hand is also present in the 'Attempt at an intimation of the allegory of Psyche' in which a not very convincing interpretation of the poem as a religious treatise is given, where Satan and God war for the soul of Psyche. The word 'Attempt' in the title of the piece perhaps suggests that Theodosia unconsciously knew that she was bending the interpretation of the poem to suit her own religious beliefs. Mary's last moments are described as only Theodosia would wish to relate them:

. . . many days before her death she frequently uttered the mournful lamentation, 'Thy rebukes have broken my heart,' and thirty-six hours before her departure, in the presence of her husband, her mother, her brother, and her affectionate attendant, she cheered their departing souls by assuring them, with a most animated countenance, that her terrors of death were entirely removed and that she felt God with the strength of her heart, and *would be her portion for ever and ever and ever.*[9]

This tiny book is less loving as a tribute than her *Observations* on the journal of her daughter. But in the last pages of *Reflections*, Theodosia quotes in full William's last word on Mary – his poem in reply to her plea not to forget her in 'On Receiving a Branch of Mezereon'. His response takes the form of a poem which now can be seen engraved on a tablet on the wall of the mausoleum. This is the 'oblong-square' which William Howitt found empty when he went to do his research for her biography thirty-six years after her death. Howitt's ghost may perhaps be appeased by the correct placing of the tribute and by the resolution of some of the 'strangely clashing accounts' of Mary Tighe. Facing the door above the recumbent figure with her guardian angel is Mary's name with her husband's and her parents' names inscribed below:

## MARY TIGHE

Wife of Henry Tighe of Kilcarry, Co. Carlow,
and daughter of the
Revd Wm. Blachford and Theodosia Tighe his wife.
She died at Woodstock in this parish
on the 24th day of March 1810, in the 37th year of her age.

> If on this earth she passed in mortal guise
> A short and painful pilgrimage, shall we,
> Her sad survivors grieve, that love divine
> Removed her timely to perpetual bliss?
> Thou art not lost! In chastest song and pure
> With us still lives thy virtuous mind and seems
> A beacon for the weary soul, to guide
> Her safely through affliction's winding path,
> To that eternal mansion gained by thee.
>
> *W.T.*

William's initials stand out clearly at the end of the poem. He suffered at her loss and in the sadness of the latter years of her life. He wrote as a way of assuaging his grief at the recognition of Mary's unhappiness, the memory of first love – and the very shortness of it all. The words stand out upon the walls of the mausoleum in sharp relief. 'Thou art not lost!'

NOTES

1 Mary Tighe: *Reading Journal*, 1806-09  NLI 4804.
2 'I Saw Thy Form in Youthful Prime', Thomas Moore, 1811.
3 'The Grave of a Poetess', Felicia Hemans, 1827.
4 Letter to John Lodge from Felicia Hemans, July 1831 at The Hermitage, Kilkenny.
5 ibid.
6 'Written after Visiting a Tomb near Woodstock in the County of Kilkenny' by Felicia Hemans, 1831.

7 *National Lyrics and Songs for Music, 1834* written in 1831 by Felicia Hemans and published in National Lyrics and Songs for Music 1834.

8 Poem written by Caroline Hamilton in 1859 and sent to Fanny Webber (née Kelly). Extracted from the memoir of Isabella Francis Wingfield, 24 December 1860: NLI Genealogical Office.

9 *Mary, A Series of Reflections During Twenty Years*, NLI LO 373.

# Sources

Nᴀᴛɪᴏɴᴀʟ Lɪʙʀᴀʀʏ ᴏғ Iʀᴇʟᴀɴᴅ, Dᴜʙʟɪɴ  (NLI)
Extracts from a Journal of M.B. born 1772, Ms 4810
Observations on the Journal of Mary Tighe by Theodosia Blachford, Ms 4810
Mary Tighe by Caroline Hamilton, Ms 4810
Reminiscences of Caroline Hamilton, Ms 4811
The 1798 Rebellion in Ireland. Letters  April-Nov. 1798. Ms 4813
The Brompton Volumes, Ms 5495, Box A
Mss  3889, 4800, 4801, 4803, 4804, 4809
Selena, Mss 4742-46
Mary, A Series of Reflections during Twenty Years, Ms LO373

Pᴜʙʟɪᴄ Rᴇᴄᴏʀᴅ Oғғɪᴄᴇ ᴏғ Nᴏʀᴛʜᴇɴ Iʀᴇʟᴀɴᴅ, Dᴜʙʟɪɴ (PRONI)
Tighe family papers, including letters Mss D2685/1-15

Bᴏᴅʟᴇɪᴀɴ Lɪʙʀᴀʀʏ, Oxғᴏʀᴅ
Mary Tighe: Psyche; or, The Legend of Love, Vet.A6 f214.

Tʜᴇ Bʀɪᴛɪsʜ Lɪʙʀᴀʀʏ
Mary Tighe: Psyche; or, The Legend of Love, General Reference Collection C.95.b.38.
(Copy 2) General Reference Collection C.150.c.2.
William Tighe: The Plants, General Reference Collection SFX lsidyv3c5e4cdb.

Quotations from Mary Tighe's poetry are taken from Harriet Kramer Linkin's edition *The Collected Poems and Journals of Mary Tighe* (University Press of Kentucky, 2005) by kind permission of the Editor.

# Bibliography

Brown, Sue, *Joseph Severn. A Life. The Rewards of Friendship*. OUP, 2009

Buchanan, Averill, *Mary Blachford Tighe. The Irish Psyche.*Cambridge Scholars Publishing, 2011

Burke, Sir Bernard, *Landed Gentry of Ireland*. Harrison and Sons, London, 1912

Burtchaell, George Danes and Thomas Ulick Sadleir, *Alumni Dublinenses*. Williams and Norgate, 1924

Carpenter, Andrew, *Verse in English from Eighteenth-Century Ireland*. Cork University Press, 1998

Clarke, Sheila, *Writers in Residence*. Ashford Books, 2006

Craig, Maurice and Michael Craig, *Mausolea Hibernica*. The Lilliput Press, Dublin, 1999

Crookshank Anne and The Knight of Glin, *The Watercolours of Ireland 1690-1914*. Barrie & Jenkins, London, 1994

Crookshank, C.H., *Memorable Women of Irish Methodism*. Wesleyan Methodist Book Room, City Road, London, 1882

——, *History of Methodism in Ireland, Vols I & II*. T. Woolmer, City Road, London, 1886

Crotty, Patrick (ed.), *The Penguin Book of Irish Poetry*. Penguin Classics, 2010

Curnock, N., *The Journal of John Wesley*. The Epworth Press, London, 1938

Daniel, Thomas, *Captain of Death. The Story of Tuberculosis*. University of Rochester Press, 1997

Day, Angelique (ed.), *Letters from Georgian Ireland. The Correspondence of Mary Delany 1731-68*. Friar's Bush Press, Belfast, 1991

De Jong, (ed.), *The Diary of Elizabeth Richards (1798-1825). From the Wexford Rebellion in Ireland to family life in the Netherlands*. Jesselstein Hilversum, Verloren, 1999

Dowden, Wilfred S., *The Journal of Thomas Moore*. Associated University Presses, 1983

Doyle, Danny and Terence Folan, *The Gold Sun of Irish Freedom, 1798 in Song and Story*. Mercier Press, 1998

Dunne, Tom, *Rebellions*. The Lilliput Press, 2004

Eger, Elizabeth and Lucy Peltz, *Brilliant Women. 18th-Century Bluestockings*. National Portrait Gallery London, 2008

Finney, Claude Lee*, The Evolution of Keats's Poetry*. New York: Russell and Russell, 1936

Forsaith, Peter, *The Romney Portrait of John Wesley*. Methodist History 42:4 (July 2004)

Foster, R.F., *Modern Ireland 1600-1972*. Penguin, 1989

——, *Oxford Illustrated History of Ireland*. OUP, 1989

Green, Dudley, *Patrick Brontë, Father of Genius*. The History Press, 2010

Hamilton, C.J., *Notable Irishwomen*. Sealy, Briars and Walker, 1904

Harrison G. Elsie, *The Clue to the Brontës*. Methuen & Co, 1948

Hayden, Ruth, *Mrs Delany. Her Life and Flowers*. British Museum Press, 2006

Hepworth Dixon, W., *Lady Morgan's Memoirs: Autobiography, Diaries and Correspondence, Vol. 1*. William H. Allen and Co, London, 1862

Howitt, William, *The Homes and Haunts of the British Poets*. Routledge, 1847 and 1894

Idle, Christopher, *The Journal of John Wesley. Abridged*. Lion Publishing plc, 2003

Kelly, Linda, *Ireland's Minstrel*. I.B.Tauris & Co. Ltd, 2006

Kirwan, John (ed.), *Reminiscences of Marianne-Caroline Hamilton (1777-1861)*. OLL Editions, Castlegarden, Thomastown, Co. Kilkenny, 2009

——, *William Tighe: Statistical Observations relative to the County of Kilkenny made in the years 1800 and 1801. Vols 1& 2, first published 1802*. Grange Silver Publications, Kilkenny, 1998

Kramer Linkin, Harriet, *The Collected Poems and Journals of Mary Tighe*. University Press of Kentucky, 2005
*Selena, by Mary Tighe*. Ashgate, 2012

Kucich, Greg, *Keats, Shelley and Romantic Spenserianism*. Pennsylvania State University Press, 1991

Lightbown, Mary, *Memorial to a Poetess: John Flaxman's Monument to Mary Tighe*. Old Kilkenny Review, 1993

Longford, Elizabeth, *Wellington: The Years of the Sword*. Weidenfeld and Nicolson, 1969

Mavor, Elizabeth, *The Ladies of Llangollen.* Penguin, 1973

Mays Jim, *The Lyrical Ballads in Wicklow.* The Coleridge Bulletin, Spring, 1998

McBride, Ian, *Eighteenth-Century Ireland.* Gill & Macmillan, 2009

McCarthy, Denis, *Dublin Castle: At the Heart of Irish History.* Government of Ireland, 2004

Moorman, Lewis J., *Tuberculosis and Genius.* University of Chicago Press, Illinois, 1940

Motion, Andrew, *Keats.* Faber & Faber, 1997

Munk, William, *The Life of Sir Henry Halford.* Longmans Green, London, 1895

O'Brien, Conor, The Byrnes of Ballymanus. Wicklow History Society Journal, Spring, 1998

O'Donnell, Ruan, *The Rebellion in Wicklow 1798.* Irish Academic Press, 1998

Owens Blackburne, E., *Illustrious Irishwomen, Vols I & II.* Tinsley Brothers, London, 1877

Pakenham, Eliza, *Tom, Ned and Kitty.* Phoenix, 2007

Pakenham, Thomas, *The Year of Liberty.*Weidenfeld and Nicolson, 1997

Robins, Joseph*, Champagne and Silver Buckles. The Viceregal Court at Dublin Castle 1700-1922.* The Lilliput Press, Dublin, 2001

Roe, Nicholas, *John Keats and the Culture of Dissent.* Oxford, Clarendon Press, 1997

Ross, Marlon B., *The Contours of Masculine Desire. Romanticism and the Rise of Women's Poetry.* Oxford University Press, 1986

Rousseau, Jean-Jacques, *Emile or On Education.* (Introduction, Translation and Notes. Allan Bloom). HarperCollins Basic Books, 1979

Stott, Anne, *Hannah More. The First Victorian.* OUP, 2003

Weller, Earle Vonard, *Keats and Mary Tighe.* The Century Co. For the Modern Languages Association of America. New York, 1928

Whyte, Thomas J., *The Story of Woodstock.* Cappagh Press, Dublin, 2007

Wordsworth, Jonathan, *The Bright Work Grows.* Woodstock Books, Washington DC, 1997

——, *Ancestral Voices, Visionary Gleam.* Woodstock Books, London and New York 1991, 1993

Wu, Duncan (ed), *Romantic Women Poets, An Anthology.* Blackwell Publishers, 1997

Yeldham, Charlotte, *Maria Spilsbury Taylor.* Irish Architectural and Decorative Studies (Journal of the Irish Georgian Society) Volume 8, 2005

——, *Maria Spilsbury Taylor.* Ashgate, 2010

# Illustrations

*Chapter 3*

1 Elevation of Parliament House, Dublin by Peter Mazell based on the drawing by Rowland Omer 1767.
2 View of The Great Courtyard, Dublin Castle 1792 by James Malton. This image is reproduced courtesy of The National Library of Ireland (PD3181).
3 William Tighe (1766-1816) by George Romney. Reproduced by permission of the Provost and Fellows of Eton College.
4 Sarah Tighe, copy of portrait by Maria Spilsbury Taylor, artist unknown: private collection.
5 *Education* by Caroline Hamilton: private collection.

*Chapter 4*

1 The drawing room at Rossana by Maria Spilsbury Taylor: private collection.
2 John Wesley preaching under a tree 1786 in Ireland by Maria Spilsbury Taylor reproduced with the permission of The Trustees of Wesley's Chapel, City Road, London.
3 Henry Tighe and Mary Blachford by Henry Brooke: private collection.

*Chapter 5*

1 Henry Tighe, after George Romney: courtesy of Antony Tighe.
2 The Pleasure Gardens at Vauxhall by Thomas Rowlandson.
3 Mary Tighe by George Romney. Photograph courtesy of the National Gallery of Ireland.
4 The Ladies of Llangollen by Lady Leighton.
5 Mrs Siddons and Philip Kemble in *Macbeth*.
6 Plas Newydd, Llangollen, photograph, the author.
7 Lady Elizabeth Fownes and Sir William Fownes by an unknown artist: courtesy of Antony Tighe.
8 Anna Seward by Tilly Kettle.
9 Valle Crucis Abbey: photograph, the author.
10 Rossana Cottage, 1883, courtesy of Irish Architectural Archive.

*Chapter 7*

1 The Death of Wolfe Tone by Walter C. Mills. This image is reproduced courtesy of The National Library of Ireland. (*Irish Weekly Independent*, December 1897.)

2  Piking the Loyalists on Wexford Bridge, by George Cruickshank, 10 June 1798. This image is reproduced courtesy of The National Library of Ireland. (HP 1798 12(c)).

3  Rossana House under Siege by Caroline Hamilton: private collection.

*Chapter 8*

1  Hamwood House, home of Charles and Caroline Hamilton: photograph, Sue Townsin.

2  The Gentleman Farmer by Caroline Hamilton: private collection.

3  Drawing of Psyche from a Bodleian Library copy of *Psyche; or, The Legend of Love* by kind permission of The Bodleian Libraries, The University of Oxford (Vet.A6 f214 p.61).

4  The drive at Rossana: photograph, the author.

*Chapter 9*

1  Portrait of Hannah More by John Opie: by kind permission of the Mistress and Fellows, Girton College, Cambridge.

2  An appointments list from the pocket-book of Dr Vaughan: ©The Royal College of Physicians, London.

3  Portrait of Sir Henry Halford by Sir Thomas Lawrence c. 1825–30. © The Royal College of Physicians, London.

*Chapter 10*

1  John Keats by Joseph Severn from H. Buxton Forman's 1883 edition of Keats's poetry.

2  The Dying Keats by Joseph Severn from H. Buxton Forman's 1883 edition of Keats's poetry.

*Chapter 11*

1  Letter to Mrs Wilmot, a poem. From *Psyche; or, The Legend of Love* by kind permission of The Bodleian Libraries, University of Oxford (Vet.A6 f.214).

2  Sydney Owenson, Lady Morgan by René Théodore Berthon, courtesy of The National Gallery of Ireland.

3  Thomas Moore, after Sir Thomas Lawrence

*Chapter 12*

1  William Tighe of Rossana (1766-1816): private collection.

2  William Tighe (senior) of Rossana (1738 -82) by Pompeo Batoni: private collection.

3  The gates at Woodstock: photograph, the author.

4 Woodstock with the extensions added by William Tighe in the early 1800s: courtesy of Antony Tighe.

5 A newly erected replica of the conservatory at Woodstock: photograph, the author.

*Chapter 13*

1 Mary's harp: courtesy of Seamus Corballis: photograph, the author.

2 The Nore at Inistioge seen from the path leading down from Woodstock: photograph, the author.

3 Figures carved on the pillar of the harp: courtesy of Seamus Corballis, photograph, the author.

4 Inscription on the harp: Sebastian Erard, 18 Great Marlborough Street: courtesy of Seamus Corballis: photograph, the author.

*Chapter 14*

1 Gardening at Woodstock: photograph, Antony Hurst.

2 Winter-flowering daphne, or mezereon.

*Chapter 15*

1 Detail of the figure at Mary's shoulder on her tomb: photograph, the author.

2 Inscription – poem by William Tighe on the wall of the mausoleum: photograph, the author.

# Index